Strange Tales of Scotland

Strange Tales of Scotland

Jack's Strange Tales Book 1

Jack Strange

Contents

'How shall we sing the Lord's song: in a strange land?'
Psalms 137; 4

Introduction

This small book has stories of the unusual, the bizarre and the just plain creepy. Some are old, some are fairly modern and some contain elements of both. They have nothing much in common except that, at one time or other, people have believed them.

Scotland can be a strange country, even today, with what is unusual elsewhere being commonplace here. Intricately carved Pictish Stones sit in churchyards or beside the road; stone circles erupt from moorland or fields, mysterious brochs exist nowhere else except Scotland and until recently farmers left a corner of their fields severely alone.

These were the Devil's or Gudeman's Crofts although the tradition probably extended further back in time than any belief in the antithesis of Jesus Christ. Most of these corners were merely left neglected but in some places there were strict ceremonies. For example in Corgarff, high in Aberdeenshire, there were two such places, each surrounded by a protective dry-stane dyke. On the First of April these areas were anointed with milk, which prevented the devil from entering the house, barn or byre. Neither the farmer, or his wife, horse nor cattle were advised to cross this unhallowed piece of land in peril of invoking bad luck.

There were other methods of protecting land and beasts of course, with the most common being a rowan twig or branch placed in a prominent position to ward off fairies, witches and such like unwanted creatures. Rowan trees are still quite commonly seen near to houses, not only in the Highlands.

Sometimes even the place names of Scotland can hide strange tales. Take the town of Aberfeldy, for instance. The name comes from *Peallaidh*, the shaggy one, who was an *uruisg*. For the sake of the uninitiated, an *uruisg* was a large, hairy creature, not quite man, not quite beast, that usually lived near a waterfall. In this case *Peallaidh* was thought to be the king of the *uruisgs* and lived at the spectacular Falls of Moness a few miles from Aberfeldy. One wonders if the belief in *uruisgs* was a folk memory of the time before homo-sapiens, when other types of human roamed the land.

While the *uruisg* was fairly benign, there were creatures that were best avoided, such as the horrendous *Cu-saeng* that infested the Parbh near Cape Wrath in the very north west of Scotland. It was one of the most mysterious horrors to haunt the country and was also reputed to be on Rannoch Moor and the inner wastes of the Grampians. However, because of its predatory nature, nobody could describe it, because nobody saw it and lived. The closest anybody got was one fortunate traveller who saw its shadow on a remote hill – and swore that it had two heads. Another walker once found huge footprints in the snow near Cape Wrath, which brings echoes of Bigfoot or the yeti. One wonders if this thing is related to the Big Grey Man of Ben MacDhui.

Such stories may yet be proved to have at least an element of truth. Some people believed that Long Tam Dalyell was in league with the devil; some people saw the strange skeletal beings that danced at the wedding of King Alexander III; people actually witnessed the Egyptian bone launch itself through the air in an Edinburgh flat; there might well have been cannibals along the Ayrshire coast or on the fringes of the Highlands, many castles have a strange atmosphere and the lighthouse keepers on the Flannan Islands undoubtedly did disappear without trace.

So if there is just a small element of truth in these tales, they have the ability to unsettle a little. If they are entirely true – and the story of the Big Grey Man of Ben MacDhui is in itself supported by some very creditable witnesses - they could leave the reader wondering if there is more to Scotland than meets the eye, and could leave him or her wondering if the scientists do, after all, have all or indeed any of the answers. So read on, and prepared to have a very uncomfortable feeling when you finish this small book and walk the bens, glens and streets of Scotland.

Spectre at the Wedding

Looking back through the brawling pages of Scottish history, it may seem inevitable that this small northern nation should have struggled for very survival when its southernmost neighbour is arguably the most aggressive state in Europe. After all, every one of England's neighbours suffered from her propensity for invasion: why should Scotland be any different? What is even more intriguing is why the Scots should have trusted Edward Plantagenet of England sufficiently to invite him to arbitrate on the foxed question of the Scottish royal succession at the hinder end of the thirteenth century. In hindsight, trusting a Mediaeval English king was like putting a head in a crocodile's mouth and then asking if it was hungry. Yet that is what the Scots did in the 1280s, and the result was centuries of some of the bloodiest, most bitter warfare in Europe, if not in the world. And it was all caused by a man's love for a woman.

He was no ordinary man, of course, but a royal. He was King Alexander III, known as Alexander the Good, whose reign was the last Golden Age Scotland was to enjoy for centuries. He was a strong king who defeated a major Norwegian invasion at the Battle of Largs and wrested the Hebrides back to Scotland. He was a strong king who refused to pay homage for his kingdom to the deviously cunning Henry III of England. Indeed if Alexander had survived, Edward Longshanks might never have tried to impose English rule on Scotland and relations between the two nations would have been far easier, even today.

However, even strong kings have human weaknesses, and Alexander's was as human as they get. His first wife, Margaret, daughter of Henry III of England, bore him three sickly children, but they all died within a few years of the death of their mother, leaving Alexander with neither a wife nor an heir. Both these items were essential for a mediaeval king, and so Alexander cast his eye around for somebody suitable. He needed lusty woman who was capable of bearing him sons, and found her in the fair Yolande de Dreux, Duchess of Brittany, a French noblewoman who fitted the bill perfectly.

It was originally Alexander's plan to marry in Kelso Abbey, but Scotland's most significant seer, True Thomas of Ercildoune, had a dream in which the roof of Kelso collapsed on its assembled congregation. Accordingly the king altered his plans and chose Jedburgh Abbey instead, only a few miles away across the green Border countryside. People tended to listen to True Thomas, for his predictions had a knack of being correct. He had already foreseen the Scottish victory at Largs, despite the lack of experience of the Scottish army, and he spoke of other events that had not yet come to pass. His prediction about Kelso came true too, but not for a few hundred years when the abbey roof collapsed in the eighteenth century.

So Jedburgh it was, and the splendid building beside the Jed Water saw a magnificent royal wedding. It was a significant occasion, and, according to Walter Bower's *Scottichronicon*, written around 1440, there was a sword dance, surely one of the first recorded, but it was neither that nor the bagpipes that was the main topic of conversation.

There was a masque ball as part of the celebrations, and amongst the happy guests, True Thomas saw the sinister shape of dancing skeletons. Others may also have seen the same thing, or at least a solitary figure that they were unable to decide was a man or a ghost. Some accounts speak of women screaming and knights crossing themselves against the dark arts. Whatever it was that appeared before the elite of Scotland that day, it seemed to glide rather than walk, and certainly was not a good omen.

People might have looked to True Thomas for an explanation, but seers seldom can explain their visions. They just see and speak and let the world take its own course. There were as many tales about Thomas as tales he told, and most were complete fabrications. People said he had visited Fairyland through a door in the Eildon Hills. People said the Fairy queen gave him the gift of prophesy in return for his prowess as a lover. People said he could never tell a lie. People tend to say ridiculous things on a whim.

But for the moment, Alexander forgot about Scotland's most famous seer and concentrated on his new wife. As was common among royalty, affairs of state kept them apart from time to time, and on one dark spring day, Alexander was in Edinburgh while Yolande was in Fife. He wanted to get back to his wife, but all his court advised otherwise. They looked at the weather, looked at the heaving waves of the Firth of Forth and shook their collective head.

If Alexander had listened to True Thomas when he thought it best not to marry in Kelso, he should have listened to him that day, for the seer uttered the prophesy that foretold the next few centuries of Scotland's history.

'On the morrow, afore noon, shall blow the greatest wind that ever was heard before in Scotland'

Ignoring all the good advice, Alexander pulled rank and forced the always-independent Forth ferrymen to pull him across the mile or two of white-frothed water of what was then known as the Scotswater or the Scottish Sea. Now it is called the Firth of Forth but on a blowy day the waves still hammer at the shore and the wind can make walking the shore an adventure and sailing perilous.

Doubtless grumbling under their breath, the ferrymen did as the king commanded, and everyone would be relieved when they reached the north shore and the king could scramble on to Fife. He would have scoffed at the doubters, for all he had to do now was ride the handful of miles along the coast and he would be safe in the arms of his wife, where he belonged.

Accordingly he took horse and headed east, but somewhere along the high road that followed the line of the cliff between Kinghorn and Burntisland, His Grace slipped and fell. His body was found next morning and all of Scotland mourned.

A rhyme of the period said;

'*When Alexander our king was dead*
That Scotland led in luwe and le
Away was sons of ale and brede
Off wyne and wax, off gamyn and glee

Our gold was changed into lede
Cryste born into virginyte
Succour Scotland and remede
That stad in its perplexte'

The people were right to mourn, and True Thomas was right about the storm. It had been threatening ever since English kings decided they should add Scotland to their dominions, and now the clouds mounted above the hazed horizon of the mediaeval nation. Without a definite heir, and with a number of claimants all eager to sit on the Scottish throne because of some trick of their birth, the Scots were unsure who to choose. Trusting that Edward Longshanks was a truly chivalrous knight, the Scots asked him to arbitrate in selecting their next king. He agreed, with the proviso that he should be Overlord. Believing the alternative was civil war, the Scots agreed.

The rest is too well known to detail. Edward chose John Baliol as Scotland's monarch and bullied him until that much-slandered man rose against the Plantagenet king. A veteran English army ravaged Berwick and massacred the inhabitants, smashed the Scottish feudal host at Dunbar and occupied the country. Defeat appeared total and irrevocable, but Scotland is not a nation to take for granted. Reeling, a new Scotland emerged, a Scotland of Wallace and the Black Douglas, of guerrilla warfare and Robert the Bruce. Decades of war followed famine and more war, as what had been a peaceful and fairly prosperous nation faced a world in which a man's worth was judged by the size of his fighting tail, and warfare became a way of life.

And what became of True Thomas? Legend says he was in his tower of Ercildoune when a white hind and stag appeared outside. Knowing what it meant, he left the tower and followed them, straight back into the arms of his Fairy Queen. He may well be at peace there, but Queen Yolande is certainly not. Sometimes she can still be seen, walking around the base of the Celtic cross that was erected to mark the spot where her husband died.

Monsters at the Loch

Of all the monster legends in the western world, that of Loch Ness is probably the best known. This stretch of dark water in the north of Scotland attracts thousands of tourists, year after year, there have been dozens of books written, a few films made, tens of thousands of photographs taken and about as many newspaper articles either deriding or analysing the phenomena of the loch. There are professional 'monster hunters' and people equally desperate to prove the whole thing is a hoax: yet despite all the publicity and the hype nobody can yet finally prove the existence or otherwise of this so called monster.

The first recorded sighting of a strange creature in this area was in the sixth century AD when Saint Columba came east from Iona to spread the Word of Christianity to the pagan Brude, King of the Picts near Inverness. Adomnan, Columba's biographer, wrote of the supernatural conflict between Columba and Broichan, who was Brude's personal druid as well as his foster father. What may have impressed even the druid was an encounter outside the dun of the king. A large creature arose from the River Ness and was ready to close its huge jaws on the head of an innocent bystander when Columbus raised his hand and shouted. Columba's voice, or the Word of God, was enough to scare the creature into a hastily withdrawal.

Broichan may have been put out by this blatant display of Christian power in his own back yard, so he predicted that a storm would batter the saint on his return to his west. The prediction was proved correct, but as Columba lived on a Hebridean island he was used to foul weather and returned home safely. Anyway it was a pretty safe bet to predict stormy weather in western Scotland: it would have been more impressive had Broichan said there would be a lasting spell of fair weather.

That was not only the first known mention of a monster in the region of Loch Ness; it was also the first mention of magic there: both seen intertwined in the legend of Nessie, the familiar name for the Loch Ness Monster. The Gaelic speaking locals called her *An Niseag* – the Scots pronunciation would be *neeshack*. Yet there is a silent message that may hint at ancient knowledge. At Balmacaan, not far from the loch, there is a stone with carvings that long predate the memory of man. These carvings show some strange beast that might be a snake, or something very much larger. It may be Nessie, or it may not. Like so much here, there is more mystery than hard fact.

Although the legend of Nessie is old, sightings seem to have been remarkably infrequent. There was apparently mention of it in the sixteenth century, which was also a time of great religious upheavals and of witch trials so people were receptive to strange ideas. In the following century *Blaeu's Atlas*, published in 1653 does not mention a monster but records: 'waves without wind, fish without fin and a floating island' all of which are unusual at least. It would appear that there was something different about the loch, but nothing spectacular: yet.

So the monster, if monster she is, was remarkably quiet but there were local tales about another creature, a water horse that waited at the side of the loch for the unwary to jump on its back, whereupon it would gallop into the water and kill the unfortunate rider. As with most of these tales, there was never anything specific, only rumours and legends, dark mutterings as winter closed in on the surrounding hills and warnings of danger by the deep water.

In the early nineteenth century the loch was disturbed as engineers decided to create the Caledonian Canal to facilitate passage between the East and West coast of Scotland. Perhaps the sound of more vessels with steam paddle ships joining the ghosting vessels of sail wakened the creature, as she raised her unwelcome head on more than one occasion that century. Or perhaps it was not the monster but the water horse that was seen dimly through the haze of half-belief and fear.

There was also the occasional accident as men fell overboard from boats, such as the shepherd Duncan MacLaren who drowned in February 1860, and Edward Murphy, a drummer in the Cameron Highlanders who sailed a small boat in the loch in July 1885. It capsized in calm water without cause or explanation. Some thought that the loch would demand a death and spoke of the old days when animals and perhaps children were sacrificed to the spirit of the water or to long-forgotten gods banished by the Cross of Columba.

Others were luckier: one near escape occurred on the 31st March 1829 when a funeral party were travelling from Inverness to the old church at Boleskine. One chaise was passing the Black Rock at Inverfarigaig when, for no accountable reason, the driver of a post-chaise decided to leave his post, the coach overturned and slid toward the loch. It only halted when it ran against some birch trees. In exactly the same area in June 1831 the congregation of Boleskeine church were alarmed by a sudden change in the weather and hurriedly ran outside, to be met by what they termed a 'waterspout' that carried away a number of barns and immersed them waist deep in water. Boleskeine was like that: strange things happened there.

There was an occasional shipwreck, such as *Commodore* of Greenock with a cargo of oatmeal which capsized in a sudden squall in January 1853. The master, Captain Colquhoun, and crew abandoned and the vessel was later discovered afloat but drifting close to rocks at Inverfarigaig, not far from Boleskeine. Colquhoun succeeded in salvaging his ship.

Strange things continued to happen: each one insignificant in itself but when taken together the sum of the parts was more than equal to the mysterious whole. In December 1856 the *Inverness Courier* reported that there was a very 'voracious pike' that ate thirteen ducks at the west end of the loch in a single day and a number of turkeys shortly after. In August 1863 the local people were astonished when the salmon in the loch suddenly decided to race up river at the Ness Salmon fisheries. Either they knew that a storm was coming, or something chased them. And all the time the normal life of the loch side communities continued, farming, fishing, hunting, living, loving and dying.

In January 1865 the body of a small boy was found washed up on the beach at Bona Ferry. The baby was tied up in an apron, with a heavy stone to weigh him down so he would sink. As rumours spread about their character, all the local unmarried women met in the Free Church at Lochend, where a minister guaranteed that they were 'beyond reproach.' A Doctor Campbell travelled from Inverness and medically examined the breasts of the local women, then stated that none had recently given birth, so a reward of £5 was offered for any information that might lead to the mother being discovered. The case, and the treatment of the local women, caused a stir far beyond Scotland as people argued that it was immoral for women to have to so publicly prove their chastity. Beyond the public outcry, the death of the child was quietly forgotten.

So Loch Ness had its share of drownings, a case of infanticide and some creature that ate water-fowl, but there was very little public mention of a monster. That does not mean that the locals did not have their own tales and their own local knowledge. These Gaelic speaking Highlanders would not divulge too much to visitors, so what they knew normally died with them. However it seems that some snippets seeped out, so that it is known that the people who lived along the banks of Loch Ness spoke about the water-horse, which would take any unwary rider on a death dive beneath the dark waters of the loch.

Few more precise stories were heard. However there was Alexander Macdonald, who in 1802 mentioned that he had seen a mysterious beast like a salamander. Naturally he was the subject of ridicule long after, which could have hidden nervousness, or dissuaded others from admitting that they, too, had seen something strange. If other of the locals had seen anything out of the ordinary, they kept it within their own circle: what happened by the Ness stayed by the Ness.

The outside world did not know about the creature in the loch. There was silence until the 1930s, and then came a sudden surge of sightings and stories. Perhaps it was because of road building operations on the north of the loch, or perhaps there was another, more sinister reason, but Nessie became visible. On the 22nd July 1933 Mr and Mrs George Spicer were driving past the loch when something crossed the road in front of their car. They reported it as a 'most extraordinary form of animal, about ... twenty five feet long, with a long neck. At that time there had been no media publicity about any sort of monster and no reason for a visitor to announce the observation of a strange creature.

The next known sighting came the following year when Arthur Grant was riding his motor bike and nearly collided with a very similar beast as he passed the north-east shore of the loch. Then there was Margaret Munro, who that same year saw a creature with a long neck, small head and skin like an elephant.

Now that public interest was aroused, the deception began. The best known was a short film clip in 1934. This is probably the most famous image of the monster and shows a small head on a long neck apparently thrusting from the dark waters of the loch. It was also a hoax. The *Daily Mail* had hired a big game hunter named Marmaduke Wetherall to hunt down Nessie, and had mocked his failure. In revenge Wetherall created a false image and had it filmed. He could not have reckoned on the almost immediate world-wide interest.

Around the same time a circus man named Bertram Mills prepared a cage in which to hold Nessie, with a bribe of £20,000 for the person who caught her, until the police defended her by saying it was illegal to shoot or trap the creature. The chief constable may have prevented a horde of trigger-happy monster-hunters from all across the world blasting at all and sundry around the loch.

There have been other films and a number of photographs, few of which are clear enough to depict anything reliable. For example there was a South African visitor in 1938 who reputedly filmed Nessie for a full three minutes, but only a single still image has been released.

There was the 1960 film made by Tim Dinsdale: some people thought it showed a creature with humps and fins: others said it was only a boat. In 2007 came a film of what was described as a 'jet black thing, about 45 feet long.' The film maker, however, has also claimed that fairies are real. Perhaps they are.

But Nessie, under whatever name, is not the only disturbing thing about Loch Ness. At the beginning of the twentieth century, just before the modern wave of monster stories began, a man who was dubbed the 'most wicked' in the world took up residence on the shores of the loch. Aleister Crowley was born in Leamington Spa into the Plymouth Brethren, a strict branch of Christianity. In common with many middle class boys, he was sent to a boarding school, where he was bullied by masters and tortured by the pupils who delighted in punching him in his kidneys as soon as they learned he had a kidney disorder: again that was not an uncommon experience for those who did not fit in such places. Crowley became a rebel against his strictly Christian mother, his repressive uncle and his tormenting school.

As an adult he travelled extensively and experimented with various spiritual ideas, becoming more and more immersed in magic and the occult. The press learned about him and called him 'the most evil man in Britain.' There were rumours of Satanism. One book Crowley owned was a mediaeval volume named *Book of the Sacred Magic of Abraham the Jew* which claimed that a Guardian Angel was appointed to every human when they were born. There was a ceremony, the Abramelin Operation that would enable anybody to tap into the magical knowledge of his or her guardian angel. However the ceremony was long and complex and would work only in certain locations. One such place was Boleskine House, by the shores of Loch Ness, which, according to Crowley's own words was:

a house where proper precautions against disturbance can be taken; this being arranged, there is really nothing to do but to aspire with increasing fervor and concentration, for six months, towards the obtaining of the Knowledge and Conversation of the Holy Guardian Angel ... There should be a door opening to the north from the room of which you make your oratory. Outside this door, you construct a terrace covered with fine river sand. This ends in a "lodge" where the spirits may congregate.

Boleskine house was a long white eighteenth century mansion. It had originally been named Boleskine Lodge and was allegedly built to anger the local landlord, Simon Fraser: he had supported the Hanoverians during the 1745 Rising that saw so many Highlanders murdered for their support of the rival Jacobite dynasty. For this act of near-treason he was not the most popular person on the loch side.

There was also a story that the house has a tunnel to the local grave-yard where witches were once said to prance and cast their spells. Crowley thought it a 'Thelemic Kiblah' or a 'Magical East' which was perfect for his twisted ideas. He bought into the entire Boleskine legend: a house situated in a lonely spot complete with a past thick with legend and horror. One local story claimed that the house had been built on the ruins of a Catholic church that had burned to the ground while the congregation were attending mass. Such a history would appeal to a man who rebelled in every way against his strictly Christian childhood.

Crowley apparently conducted black magic rituals at the house, hoping to bring out the four princes of evil, while others of his persuasion gathered there, made talismans to their beliefs and sacrificed goats and cats. He founded a cult he called Thelema whose motto was 'Do what thou wilt shall be the whole of the law.' The cult survives among a small number of adherents, with the odd person believing that Boleskine House is the mother fount of their belief. There were also stories of debauchery with sex and drugs. Rather than hiding his ugly practices, Crowley gloated over them in print:

The demons and evil forces had congregated round me so thickly that they were shutting off the light. It was a comforting situation.

However rather than being in Crowley's control, these evil forces seem to have run riot in the area. Crowley's autobiography boasts of the things he unleashed chasing away a housemaid and driving a workman insane, while when he scribbled the names of demons on a butcher's bill, the butcher apparently cut off his hand and bled to death. He mentioned that one of his workers, a man who had not touched drink for decades, suddenly took to the bottle and tried to murder his wife and children. Crowley's lodge keeper was alleged to have lost first his ten year old daughter and then his fifteen month old son.

All these events were personal tragedies for the people involved, but there are other rumours that claim one of Crowley's rituals went badly wrong and he loosed a demon that slid into the loch: the Loch Ness Monster. This may or may not be true, but bad things continued to happen even after Crowley left Boleskine in 1913, the year before the First World War and after thirteen years of residence there. Lights flash off and on, headless ghosts appear, windows break by themselves and one of Crowley's chairs apparently moves across the floor of its own accord. Worse was the suicide of Major Edward Grant, who in the 1960s shot himself in a room Crowley had used for his perverted practices.

Another later owner was Jimmy Page the Rock guitarist of Led Zeppelin and a devotee of Crowley. He was rarely in the house but his ownership was enough to ensure that more legends arose that black magic was practised at Boleskine House.

So there we have it: the monster of Loch Ness that was first recorded after a magic duel between Saint Columba and the local druid, a loch with a bad reputation, a house built on the site of tragedy and the return of the monster after a man dabbled with the occult.

But Boleskine is not the only haunted place by Loch Ness. A favoured site for those who wish to search for the Loch Ness Monster, Urquhart Castle has a long and impressive history, which unfortunately has ruined most of the fabric of the building. What remains, however, is still impressive and has a unique atmosphere. At its peak Urquhart was one of the largest castles in Scotland, and it probably had to be, to contain some of the most aggressive clans in the country.

Built in the early thirteenth century, Urquhart is on the north side of the loch, with a fine situation and even a car park. The castle endured English occupation in 1296, played a full part in the Wars of Independence and was taken by Clan Donald in 1545. Since 1689 it has been unoccupied. In 1692 the castle was largely destroyed to prevent the Jacobites from using it as a base. Although there do not seem to be any actual ghosts at Urquhart, the area has creepy stories enough for anybody's taste. Not far from the castle is *Cragan nam Mallachd*, the Rock of the Curses, where the witches of the glen first set eyes on the spot where they were to build the castle. The witches and warlocks held their Sabbaths on *An Clairach*, the Harp, which is a rock on the shore of the loch near Tychat. According to the old story, Satan used to come in person on May Day (now May 12th, after the calendar changes) and they danced to his harp, or possibly his Jew's harp. Interestingly, one of the symbols of the old time druids was said to be a harp, and it just possible that this legend is a folk memory of a druidic ritual. Add to that the possibility of seeing the somewhat elusive Loch Ness Monster and this spot becomes even more interesting.

Vanished

There is something romantic about a lighthouse. It may be the thought of these pencil-thin buildings standing tall and strong in middle of the ocean, daring the worst that the weather can do as they shine their warning light for night after night. Or perhaps it is the men that worked there in what must have been the loneliest and at times scariest job in the world. It would take a unique kind of man to take on that occupation, to live out there surrounded by dangerous seas, knowing that if things went wrong there was nobody to turn to, nobody to help, nobody to call...

Scottish lighthouses guard some of the worst seas in the world, with savage squalls, treacherous currents and half-hidden reefs always ready to pulp an unwary boat into matchsticks. Many have intense history, such as the Bell Rock with its tales of piracy, privateers and wartime mines, or the Sule Skerry, at the edge of three thousand miles of rolling Atlantic, where the lighthouse men were said to listen to an ethereal choir singing just beyond the horizon.

Of them all, the Flannan Islands lighthouse is arguably the most famous, simply because it was the scene of a mystery. The Flannan Islands are also known as the Seven Hunters and sit beleaguered by the growling waves of the Atlantic, some twenty miles west of the Island of Lewis in the Outer Hebrides. Before the lighthouse was built in 1899, nobody had lived here since the distant past, and since the lighthouse became automated in 1971, nobody has lived here again.

When the term 'desert island' is used, the normal image would be of a tropical atoll. There is nothing tropical about these islands; they are bleak, dour, grim and hard as they face the unrelenting force of the Atlantic breakers.

As far as can be ascertained, the only people to voluntarily live here before the lighthouse keepers were hardy Celtic monks, although even this apparent fact is disputed. The beehive shaped structures that hug the gneiss may have been used by Druids, or by seamen from Lewis who spent time collecting sea birds for feathers, flesh and eggs. Seabirds were a valuable commodity for the people of the Hebrides with the population of St Kilda virtually depending on sea birds for their survival.

The sanctity of the Flannan islands was such that those Lewis men who landed on these islands turned *deasil* – sun-wise – as soon as they arrived, then thanked God for their safe passage. They were also careful not to use certain words while they were there; these islands were considered different from other places in the Hebrides. That did not prevent them being used in the general economy, as there were also a number of sheep left to graze in this uncomfortable spot, safe from rustlers unless a passing fishing boat took a fancy to some salt-flavoured mutton.

In appearance the islands are equally unusual: they rise vertically from the sea to a height of nearly 90 metres, although spray from breaking waves often renders them all but invisible. They are not quiet islands for all their reputation for sanctity. The largest of the group is the thirty-nine acre Eilean Mor – big island- and this is where the Northern Lighthouse Board built their 74-foot high lighthouse to help guide ships away from the Flannan group and hopefully safely around Cape Wrath, the appropriately named cape of turning that marks the north west extremity of the Scottish mainland.

There were three men based on the Flannan light and right from the outset they knew it was going to be a hard posting when one man died when he fell from the light. Another four were drowned when their boat capsized and all the time the Atlantic waves pounded the cliffs and gales screamed around the light. There were bright spots though as the islands had a surprising fertility so the keepers could tend sheep and poultry to supplement their diet. And all the time the islands and the sea waited their opportunity and the spirit of the Flannans watched.

Yet the keepers kept the light shining, did their duty and guided ships to safety off that dangerous coast. There were four keepers in the crew, with three on duty at the lighthouse at any one time. They rotated their service, with two months on the light and one month at the shore station at Breascleit, Loch Roag. Such was life for the keepers: as the months passed they grew used to it, and then they vanished.

It was on the 15th December 1900 that the world first noticed something was wrong. A ship passed the islands that night and realised there was no welcoming light: all was dark on the Seven Hunters. The master reported what he had not seen but the authorities could not react. The weather was rough and there was no way of reaching the lighthouse. Anyway there was no serious cause for alarm as a fog had wrapped around the entire coast, dimming all lights. It was not until the 26th December that *Hesperus*, the relief vessel, battered through the seas to Eilean Mor. It took only minutes for Joseph Moore, the relief keeper to realise that something was seriously wrong.

There was no friendly greeting at the landing stage, no light, no reply to his increasingly frantic signals, and when he scrambled ashore, no sign of anybody on the island. Captain Jim Harvie had *Hesperus's* horn blown and the crew pointed to the lighthouse's flagpole, from which no flag flew. Moore dashed up the long staircase, opened the gate and the outer door and thrust inside the lighthouse. The clock was stopped, the beds were made, the place was all clean and tidy, the blinds were on the windows and even the cutlery was bright and clean. All was nearly as it should be, except for the lack of men.

Moore called for help and two sailors from *Hesperus* landed to search. They scoured every nook and corner of the lighthouse and found a few clues as to what might have happened. There was damage to the railings outside the cable railway and the box that held the mooring ropes at the west landing stage had completely vanished. This box had been very securely fastened to the ground and was some 120 feet above the sea. Some of the contents were found strewn among the rocks. The oilskins and sea boots of two of the keepers, James Ducat and Thomas Marshall, were missing but those of the third, Donald MacArthur, still hung forlorn from its peg.

Moore checked the log; there had been a westerly gale on the 12th and 13th of December, followed by relative calm on the 14th. The log had been filled in until nine in the morning of the 15th; then nothing. There were only blank sheets of paper. The men who were investigating that eerie lighthouse surmised that whatever had happened, had happened in the morning of the 15th.

There were many theories about what happened. Some were bizarre, such as the idea that aliens had abducted the keepers; some were ugly, such as the idea that one of the keepers had gone insane and had murdered the others before jumping into the sea himself. Some thought that a giant bird had killed all three men. There was a growing myth of a half-eaten meal and beds unmade, mainly due to the poet Wilfred Wilson Gibbon who wrote his *Flannan Isle* in 1912. Most strange of all was the half-hinted story that the spirit of the islands themselves had killed the men.

The reality is probably more prosaic. Although the main storm of the 12th and 13th had died down, the Atlantic is prone to rogue waves. It seems probable that one huge wave came just as two of the men were working at the box that held the mooring ropes. The wave washed both men away and when McArthur came to help, a following surge took him as well.

Or so the scientists and professional seamen say. However the islands were never considered as quite canny, there were always stories and perhaps, just perhaps, something else happened that day...

Monsters of the Land

The Loch Ness Monster is known around the world, but Scotland is also home to a number of even more unpleasant creatures that infest dry land. These monsters are rarely seen nowadays, perhaps because people tend to remain within the orbit of the lights of city streets, or when they do go out at night, it is within the comforting shell of a modern motor vehicle. Except for some hardy hill walkers, few people are out and alone in the real dark to meet creatures such as the terrifying *brollachan*.

This creature does not venture into towns or villages but stays in the shaded recesses of the landscape, waiting for the lonely, the vulnerable and in particular for children. Sometimes it was believed to be a part of the fairy world, or it could be the young of the *fuath*, a strange, web-footed creature that may have mated with the wildest of Highland clans in the distant and very dim past. It is also possible that humans have seen the *brollachan* but do not recognise it as it has no definite shape. It is merely a malformed mass of something, even a dark cloud on occasions, but with a pair of bright red eyes … watching. It may be less than a metre in width, or a full two metres, and apparently it is quite retiring. It dislikes trees, preferring the stark bleakness of the moors, sometimes remaining near water, which would account for the webbed feet of its parents.

This creature is best left severely alone. Although shy it is not harmless; it is a predator that eases its formless being inside a vulnerable victim, either somebody who has experienced an emotional upset, or who is depressed, or weak willed or especially young. Once inside, the *brollachan* will possess its victim and drain the life-force from it. The victim with fight back; he or she will become darker as this formless thing is within it, the victim may show wild behaviour patterns quite out of character, but it will not avail them. Unless the *brollachan* is removed, they are doomed. The *brollachan* will control them and will entice another human close, perhaps a friend or relative, and at the very time the host dies, burned out by the power of the creature that possesses him or her, the relative will be emotionally upset and therefore prone to be the next victim ... and so the pattern continues.

Naturally people did not like to be possessed by a *brollachan*, so they devised methods of driving the creature out of the victim. Unfortunately many details of the procedure have been lost, so what has come down is fragmented. It appears to be a mixture of an application of various herbs and a ritual of chanting and singing. When the *brollachan* eventually emerges, the danger is far from over as it could immediately seek another host or use its black magic on those who cast it out. Yet the *brollachan* was a creature of darkness; it feared bright light or fire; these weapons worked.

So travellers on the stark moors in the north must be aware of any shapeless mass that slithers out of the dark; look for the bright red, predatory eyes and be prepared to shine a torch directly at them ... and then run: fast.

But the *brollachan* was only one creature of the night. Perhaps not surprising given the topography and long dark winters, Scotland has a plethora of myths relating to various types of monsters, creatures and things that make the night hideously dangerous. Today most people relegate these stories to the confines of fiction, but when the dark fell at three in the afternoon and dawn was after nine the following morning, and the wind moaned through the naked branches of trees or carried only the mournful bellow of distant deer or the cry of a hunting wolf, imagination could put flesh on the bones of supernatural fear.

There were many types of dangerous creatures that seem to be peculiar to Scotland. For instance there was the *Baobhan Sith*, which was a purely feminine vampire that could be met throughout the Highlands. More specific was the *Baist Bheulach*, a creature that infested the Odal Pass, to the west of Kylerhea on the mystical, magical, unearthly Island of Skye. When the first ever road was hacked through here, the road makers were informed that the pass was infested by something that could not be properly defined. It either took the form of a man, or a dog, or a man with one leg. The workmen heard its screams and cries in the dark of the night although there does not seem to be any record of a sighting. There were tales of bodies being found and of travellers being attacked and knocked down. One theory was that this creature was the spirit of a murdered man who was looking for revenge and it seems to have sucked blood from its victims. Another theory was that the one-legged man was a folk memory of the ancient Druid seers who apparently stood on one leg to peer into the future.

Another unpleasant creature was the *Slaugh*, who were also known as the unforgiven dead. These creatures were to be avoided at all costs for they were always savage and the locals thought of them as fallen angels.

The Borders also had its share of supernatural creatures. One was the Brown Man of the Muirs. Dressed in brown, this red-haired being was said to protect the natural wildlife of the hills and moors and to attack anybody who dared hurt their charges. They were not to be mistaken for the Brownies, who could do good deeds around the house or farm in return for food. There were some who believed the Brownies were in fact Covenanters, extreme Presbyterians hunted into the wild places by government forces in the seventeenth century.

The *Cailleach Bheur* was completely different and may be a folk memory of an ancient earth goddess. She only appeared in winter, had a blue face and, like the Brown Man of the Muirs, protected animals. It seems she was a personification of a pre-Christian Goddess. She had a limited life, being born on Halloween and walked with a magical staff, which she tapped on the ground. Each tap brought the frost. However she had a limited life and on the eve of Beltane she tossed her staff under a holly bush or gorse bush and returned to stone, although in some versions she became a young maiden, presumably symbolising the birth of spring. There seem to be no surviving records of people who have actually met these creatures; they existed only in the dark recesses of folk memory, in the words of elderly people as they crowded around the bright flames of the peat-fire in the evening and in the whisper of the wind through the sodden winter heather.

There were a number of creatures which had the power to foretell a death. One was the *Caoineag*, which translates as 'the weeper.' She was found in waterfalls and howled to warn the local clan that there was a death coming, or some other terrible event. Very similar was the *Caointeach*, who was the Argyll version and also wailed to warn on coming death. The *Bodach* was another ominous creature; dark and looking like a man, its appearance also foretold of a death in the family.

The Highlands were also home to the *Cait Sith*, spiritual or ghostly cats. Some versions have the cats as large as a dog and black in colour. These animals may be a folk memory of the lynx, or perhaps only a black wild cat, a creature that is still seen in Scotland. There was also the *Cu Sith*, a green spiritual dog the size of a calf that ghosted the heather slopes, hunting for prey.

Perhaps the influx of people who tramp the Scottish hills in garish colours and who talk in loud voices have scared off the native supernatural creatures. Or perhaps the beasties are just waiting for the right opportunity to appear again.

This chapter will close with a very true story. In 1992 a family of four from Edinburgh spent a fortnight's holiday in *Gleannan t-Suidhe* in the very heart of the Island of Arran. This glen – pronounced Glen Shee - means the sacred or fairy glen and is speckled with ancient sites, with an Iron Age fort, a chambered cairn and a prominent standing stone.

The family, Michael and Katy Aitken (not their real names) with eight year old Andrew and two year old Helen, lived in a caravan right beside the standing stone, upon which Michael and the children played football. In the evening Michael would take the children up the hills while the mother grabbed a couple of hours' peace to herself. As their holiday continued the children grew weary of the nightly hill-walks and Michael walked alone.

Toward the end of the holiday he wandered as far as Loch Nuis and the lower slopes of Beinn Nuis. When he came back from the hills, Katy asked who was with him. 'Nobody' he replied but that night she woke in the caravan to see a 'tall creature without a face' beside the bed. She experienced a feeling of deep foreboding. A few moments before they left for the ferry the following day Katy broke a tendon in her leg, which still bothers her, nearly quarter of a century later. They have not returned.

There does not seem to be any specific folklore attached to Loch Nuis, but Beinn Nuis was the scene of a number of aircraft crashes during the Second World War.

Scottish beasts then, can come in many shapes and sizes; some are nearly forgotten in the cultural changes of time but others may still be there, waiting their opportunity to return.

Creatures of the Water

As well as the land, Scottish rivers, lochs and seas were reputed to hold a number of various unpleasant creatures. Loch Ness is so well known that it has been dealt with in a separate section, but there are other monster haunted lochs in Scotland apart from Ness. For instance there is the creature known as Morag that may inhabit Loch Morar in Lochaber. At over a thousand feet deep, Morar is the deepest freshwater loch in the country and is also one of the largest, with over ten square miles of surface water and five islands among which Morag could hide. This creature is another that has been present for quite some time, with recorded sightings that stretch back to 1887. The area was once home to a fairly sizeable community but as usual the Clearances and the imposition of large 'sporting' estates replaced people with certain managed animals.

There have been a reported thirty sightings of Morag, including a number with multiple witnesses. In 1948, three years after the end of the Second World War, a party of people were in a boat in the loch when they saw what they called a 'serpent-like creature about twenty feet long.' Twenty years later two men in a speedboat apparently rammed her by mistake. When Morag fought back, Duncan Mc-Donnel thumped her with an oar and his companion, William Simpson, tried to shoot her with his sporting rifle. They said that she was between twenty-five and thirty feet long, with three brown humps;

whatever it was, it submerged during the battle and they did not see it again.

As usual with Scottish creatures, earlier reports are contradictory. Some say that Morag was regarded as an omen of death, while others depict her as a form of mermaid with long hair and well developed breasts. Unlike other creatures, however, Morag was often seen in daylight, rising from the depths and moving slowly along the surface. Apparently seeing her, or hearing her wail, foretold a death in the local clan.

The island of Arran, only two hours travel from Glasgow, has Loch Iorsa. This loch has no monster although there were dark tales that the surface never ruffled even on the wildest days and at one time it was a place to be shunned. The name is said to mean loch of the snakes or adders, and legends of druids attached themselves to the loch and the glen within which it sits. It is also close to Machrie Moor on which stand some of the most impressive standing stones and stone circles anywhere.

One creature with no specific home, but which it was best to avoid was the *Bean Nighte*. This beast was always female and wore green, the Celtic mystical colour. She also had webbed feet, which proved her watery home. She could either be a warning of imminent death, or if approached properly, she could grant three wishes. Another creature with webbed feet was the *Boobrie*, which was located only in Argyll, the ancient heartland of Dalriada. The *Boobrie* was a huge black bird that swooped down to eat cattle. Even worse were the Blue Men of the Minch, who haunted the stretch of water between the Shiant Islands, which were themselves sacred, and the long island of Lewis. The Blue Men were said to live in underwater caves and were thought to wreck ships.

Waterfalls and pools were the home of the Uruisg, part human and part goat. They were not particularly dangerous and may be a folk memory of the hunter gatherers who lived in the land before the more settled Celts arrived. They could not be mistaken from the green-clothed Water Wraiths who were always female, always had haggard faces and hauled the unwary into the depths of lochs and still water.

However, of all the supernatural creatures that could be met at the waterside, the *Each Uisge* was perhaps the worst. This was the water horse, a shape shifting beast that could take the form of a beautiful horse or a handsome young man. If anybody was unwary enough to ride astride the horse, it would plunge into the water, taking the victim with him, and once beneath the surface it would eat its rider, save for the liver. If a lone woman saw a handsome man standing by the loch or river when she fetched water or was about to wash clothes, she would also be well advised to keep clear, for the same fate would befall her. Perhaps this was a method of ensuring young unmarried girls did not fall victim to the smooth talk of a young man? The water horse was also known to eat cattle or sheep.

Such a water horse was thought to haunt Loch Treig in Lochaber. The name is said to mean Loch of Death and the beast here was thought to be one of the most ferocious. It was apparently capable of both ripping the strongest man apart with its teeth and pounding him to death with its black hooves. There have been no sightings since a dam was built in 1929 and the loch became a reservoir and was used in Scotland's hydro-electricity scheme.

Another dangerous loch was Lochan-nan-Deaan on the old military road between the lonely castle of Corgarff and the planned village of Tomintoul. This loch was believed to be bottomless and to be the scene of human sacrifice long ago. An attempt to drain Lochan-nan-Deaan was said to have disturbed a red-capped spirit that threw some of the workmen into the loch and chased the others away. More accurately, when the winter closed in the road was liable to be lethal with snow and it was possible that travellers fell into the loch in the dark of night.

The Shellycoat was a water spirit from the Borders. This creature gained its name from its coat of rattling shells, which hopefully acted as a warning when it approached as it was malevolent. The Shony was another creature that was place specific, in this case the seas off the Island of Lewis, while selkies were common around many of the coasts of Scotland. Selkies could be seals at sea or humans on land. They could marry humans and breed and were among the progenitors of some Hebridean clans.

Loch na Beiste in Garloch, as the name suggests, was reputed to be the abode of a water horse or perhaps a kelpie. The loch is near to the scattered township of Mellon Udrigil, and around 1840 the proprietor of the estate, a Mr Bankes, listened to the pleas of his tenants and attempted to get rid of 'the beast.' Apparently it had been seen by a number of people recently, including Kirk elders. Mr Bankes pumped water out of the loch and checked the depth, to find it was only two metres deep; there was no sign of the beast. Many other lochs have their own stories, such as Loch Maree that was said to be home to a monster to which sacrifices were made and Loch na Fideil that had a creature that attacked women and children.

The northern isles of Orkney and Shetland have their own distinctive folklore; part Norse, part possibly from the original Pictish inhabitants. For example the Shetland Islands had a water horse known as Shoopiltee, which had the same characteristics of the Highland water horse but a different name. There was also the Noggle in Shetland, another form of water horse that was only seen near water mills, while the Morool was a multi-eyed creature of the seas.

There were mermaids of course, and there were Fin-folk. This particular breed of supernatural beings seems to be unique to Shetland and Orkney, with their headquarters, or earthly home at Eynhallow, which is an island between Mainland Orkney and the Island of Rousay. This is not a large island, being less than a third of a square mile, or 75 hectares for those who prefer the decimal equivalent. It is also uninhabited and hard to reach, with vicious tides, known as roosts, guarding the approaches. The locals know the best times to cross; anybody else may struggle. Like so much in these islands, the name is from the Norse, Eyin Helga, Holy Island.

For those who look no further than the surface, the main feature of the island is the ruins of the mediaeval church and the legend that there was once a monastery here. That would make sense, given the

Celtic church's liking for establishing holy places on remote islands: Iona and Inchcolm spring immediately to mind. At one time as many as twenty six people lived here but in 1851 the proprietor of the island cleared them after an outbreak of disease, and the island was left to the birds and the ever present Orkney winds.

Bereft of its human population, Eynhallow remained a focus of legends. It was said to be where the fin-folk spent their summer. They were safe here as they had the power to make the island invisible. However they reckoned without a farmer named the Guidman o' Thorodale, who opened the island to human occupation. He had his reasons: the Fin-folk abducted his wife so he whistled up his sons and sailed to the island. The family carved nine crosses in the ground and walked three times sunwise around the island before sowing nine rings of salt. This interesting mixture of pagan and Christian beliefs kept the island visible so that humans could find it and settle there. The Fin-folk left.

These Fin-folk were not the cheery, chattering fairies of legend, but a dark, morose people; they used magic and were disliked by the humans who lived on the surrounding islands. They could control the weather and if they took a liking to an Orcadian fisherman they could grant him fair seas; on the other hand they could call up a storm for those they disliked. Being islanders they were excellent boatmen – the Hudson Bay Company and many whaling ships sought out men from Orkney for their skills in small boats throughout the eighteenth and nineteenth centuries – but they were also shape-shifters. The Fin-folk were at home both on land and sea, creatures of earth and water in this realm and in their own.

When they were not on Eynhallow, known by them as Hildaland, they swam to Finfolkaheem, their city at the bottom of the sea. Hildaland was said to be a magical land that could not be seen by humans. The name is said to translate as 'hidden land.' Unfortunately, the Finfolk were not very pleasant neighbours for they had the nasty habit of abducting people and taking them to their undersea home. Once kidnapped, there was no return and the unfortunate victim was forced to become a husband or wife of a Fin-person. Fin-women in particular liked to have a young human male as a husband, for that was a certain way to prevent them from aging.

Fin children were said to be born as mermaids or mermen but the tails formed into legs later in life. The women were extremely attractive while the men were dark faced and brooding, so the women preferred a human husband, a match that would enable them to remain beautiful all their lives. However if they married a Fin-man they would become old and haggard.

The Orcadians believed that it was Christianity that finally removed the Fin-folk, but there was some consternation at the turn of the seventeenth and eighteenth centuries when Inuit in kayaks were driven across the Atlantic to the northern isles and some people believed that these were the Fin-folk returned. As that period coincided with a major famine in Scotland and a resurgence in witchcraft it is perhaps not surprising that there were superstitious beliefs.

There is a possibility that the Fin-folk are a corruption of the Norwegian wariness of the people of Finland, carried to the islands by Vikings and merged with the local lore of selkies or seal people. However in Orkney folklore the Fin-folk had fins that looked like human clothing. It is also possible that the invading Norse lived alongside the indigenous Picts of Orkney and miscalled them Fin-folk. The Norse would be fair haired and the Picts could be dark and naturally unhappy at this invasion of their islands, particularly given the slave-owning culture of the Norse.

Perhaps because of the Fin-folk, the island of Eynhallow was considered a magical place. Grain cut there after dark is said to bleed and horses tend to escape even if they are well tethered. For those with the power, Eynhallow has atmosphere: a feeling of something not quite canny. It is not decipherable or describable; it is just *there*, a tingling of the air, electricity in the ground, a feeling of feyness that can enter the soul and be welcomed or repelled, depending on the recipient. Strange things can happen on this small island and in 1990, a very strange thing did indeed occur. There are periodic visits to the island when a boat load of naturalists or bird watchers arrive and wander, taking photographs and examining all the delights of this scrap of northern land. On the fourteenth July 1990 a ferry landed eighty-eight bird-watchers and then left. When it returned to pick them up, there were only eighty-six people and nobody could account for the disappearance of the missing two.

The police and coastguard were informed and there was a full land and sea search with all the technology that Scotland could provide and the upshot was: nothing. The two visitors had vanished as surely as if they had never been, or as if the Fin-folk had abducted them.

There were many rumours, of course, from the simple belief that the ferry man had miscounted and there only had been eighty-six passengers all the time to the less rational who thought that the two missing people had been Fin-folk who had returned home. There were even a few people who speculated that the indigenous Fin-folk had snatched the visitors and transported them to their undersea home. Certainly no trace was ever found.

But that is perhaps typical of the waters in and around Scotland: beautiful, subject to sudden changes in mood and always with a certain air of mystery in this land that is never quite what it seems.

Caves of Death

Situated between Aberdeen and Inverness, the region of Moray is neither Highland nor Lowland but has the best of both. In the south there is moorland and the rising mountains of the Cairngorm National Park, while further north there is the fertile land of the Laigh of Moray and some of the finest coastal scenery in Scotland. This is an ancient land, redolent with standing stones and the forgotten relics of long vanished people. It has changed hands from Picts and Vikings and Scots, with the see-saw of war and the screams of battle as mailed knights rode out from strong castles and fine ladies watched from the wind-buffeted battlements.

But before the knights, before the Vikings with their long dragon ships, before the documentation of history, there were people living and dying here, and it is the dying and the manner of it that has left a chilling legacy.

To the north and slightly west of Elgin, the coast is composed of cliffs that plummet down to a gravel beach on which the sea hushes and breaks. In the middle of this beach and delving some twenty metres into the cliffs is the Sculptor's Cave. A high tide will cut the cave off, but archaeologists have found amazing and macabre reminders of Bronze Age life here: and Bronze Age death.

There are legends of human sacrifice, and for once there is evidence that may prove the old tales correct. Any casual visitor with sharp eyes can see the Pictish carvings of broken spears and leaping salmon on the rough cave walls, but archaeologists believe that these caves were occupied for hundreds or even thousands of years prior to any sort of human political organisation. Indeed it is possible that the Neolithic people used these caves.

An investigation has found a huge array of bones including a number of children's heads left over from the Bronze Age. There were around 1800 bones and pieces of bones here; one of the largest, if not the largest, collection in any Scottish cave. However the meaning of this bone collection is not known. Either it was a cave where the bodies of the dead were left to decay until the souls passed from this physical world to the next world of the spirit, or the cave was a site of human sacrifice over many hundreds of years. Scholars of the period believed that the heads of children were stuck on poles and left within or perhaps at the entrance of the cave, a line of grinning young skulls with the cranium polished to reflect the light from the hard northern sun or the gleam of moonlight off the sea: it is hard to imagine that now in this peaceful place.

Were the heads there as a warning to others of the macabre happenings within the cave? Or were they symbols of a passage into another world, signs of respect for the dead? Were they shrines to the chopped up bodies inside? That brings so many questions: who did the mutilation? Were there priests who performed these rites as a sacred religious ceremony, or perhaps the elders of the tribe? Was it done in private or public?

The shape of the cave with a longish entrance passage and a wider space inside could suggest a mother's womb so perhaps the old people saw this place as the opposite of birth, a dark passage between life and death. Reinforcing that belief is the fact that as well as bones, the caves held various objects that would be valuable in their day, such as amber beads and personal jewellery, funerary goods of the time and place. Whatever the ceremony, there is no doubt that this was an important theatre in some sort of death ritual in the Bronze Age.

More recently, a mere 1800 years or so back when the Romans were still infesting the south of Britain, this was undoubtedly a place of human sacrifice. The remains of half a dozen decapitated bodies have been found. These were perhaps prisoners of war, or men who had broken some law of the community, or they could have been chosen as human sacrifice in some religious ceremony. What is even more unsettling is the attitude to some modern visitors. There have been more recent bones found on the floor of the cave, and occasionally bundles of sticks of the type used in some practises of witchcraft, such as balefire or needfire bundles.

That begs the question: are the people who leave these items genuinely continuing the sacred practises of the cave, are they being respectful of the old ways, or have they seen *The Blair Witch Project* where a stick bundle was used and think it clever to copy that fictional film in real life?

Even yet, we are not fully aware of the reality of human sacrifice among the Celts. Most of our information comes from the writings of Romans, who met the Celtic people as bitter enemies and probably included as much propaganda as fact in their reports. However, the Romans reported that the Druids, the Celtic priests, were rumoured to sacrifice prisoners and predict the future by the way they died. Again according to outside sources, the sacred Druidical groves were the site of human as well as animal sacrifice, with pieces of intestines scattered around the trees and blood soaking into the ground. Not a pretty picture: imagine the flies.

It was Julius Caesar who recorded, or perhaps created, the incident of the Wicker Man that was made into a couple of films. In Caesar's account the Wicker Man was huge and hollow, then filled with criminals or whoever was handy and set alight. In saying that, Rome was far worse with their entire civilisation based on slavery and their public kept quiet by what they called games which were little short of public human sacrifice on a grand scale and with terrible refinements of cruelty.

The truth about Celtic human sacrifice is harder to ascertain. The pre-Christian Gaels in Ireland had a god named *Cromm Cruach* to whom children were sacrificed, at least in mythology, but as the druids ended this practise it is possible that they were against human sacrifice and Julius Caesar was merely spouting propaganda. However there are a number of Pictish carved stones that appear to show men being drowned. These may be sacrifices or perhaps a record of the demise of some prominent enemy. They may even have nothing to do with executions but represent the Cauldron of Rebirth, which was a cauldron that featured in Celtic folklore as a method of reaching the Otherworld or reviving the dead. King Arthur's quest for the Holy Grail may be a retelling of this ancient belief.

The truth about Moray's sacrificial cave will probably never be known. But if the tide is low and rising and you are hurrying along that lonely shingle beach, perhaps you may think twice before ducking into the nearest handy cave for shelter.

Mysterious Rosslyn and the Templars

Twixt the oak and the elm tree
You will find buried the millions free.

South of the capital and north of the Borders, Midlothian was once coal-mining territory and is now Edinburgh's commuter belt. It is a busy, bustling region of small towns and villages nearly linked together by residential buildings but with areas of fertile farmland and the sites of intense pastoral beauty. It is an ancient land, dotted with castles, salted with blood spilt in ancient battles, full of character and subtle mystery.

Some of the castles here are known throughout the world: Dalhousie, once home to the governor-general of India, Borthwick from where Mary Queen slipped over the wall disguised as a page-boy, Crichton, where the Scots fought an English invading force to a bloody draw and where legends of ghosts remain. But for once it is a chapel that supersedes the castles for historical interest.

Founded in the fifteenth century as the Collegiate Chapel of St Matthew, Rosslyn Chapel is near the village of Roslin on a picturesque hill overlooking Roslin Glen. The founding father was William Sinclair, the First Earl of Caithness. The story of the journey of an earl who owned land in the far north and who built such an amazing structure in Midlothian is a tale in itself, but the chapel is interesting even in its architecture. It was possibly originally intended to be only part of a larger building but without plans or an insight into Sinclair's mind, the truth will never be absolutely sure. What was built is fascinating. The Apprentice Pillar displays workmanship of the highest standard, while the representations of maize were carved half a century before Columbus apparently discovered North America, which gives rise to all sorts of speculation about Scottish voyagers crossing the Atlantic. There is the usual Christian imagery, together with a Green Man, which is less usual in Scotland than England and sometimes explained as a pre-Christian fertility or perhaps harvest symbol.

In common with other Christian religious sites in Scotland, Rosslyn followed the Roman Catholic rites until 1560, when the Scottish Reformation turned religion upside down and the reformed practises of Protestantism became more common. The chapel became a target for vandalism and anger. Cromwell's men came this way in 1650 when they besieged nearby Roslin Castle; they stabled their horses in the chapel. Strangely they did less damage than an Edinburgh mob that later rampaged through the chapel smashing some of the beautiful carvings.

For three centuries Rosslyn was closed to any sort of worship and then in 1861 the Episcopalians began to use the chapel. The local people naturally knew of the carvings and a host of attached legends, but few other people took much interest in this beautiful but small building in the heart of the countryside. That was fine and dandy and life continued without much change until Rosslyn was featured in a book named *The Da Vinci Code*. Suddenly the world realised that Scotland's romance did not only consist of tartans, clans, Mary Queen of Scots and Loch Ness; there were Knights Templar and the Holy Grail as well. But how true are the legends?

There are many myths surrounding the Knights Templar. They came into existence in 1119, which was about two decades after the

First Crusade had reclaimed Jerusalem and the Holy Land for Christendom after over four hundred years of Muslim occupation. The Temple in question was Temple Mount in Jerusalem, originally built by the Biblical Solomon and important to Jews and Muslims as well as Christians. After the re-conquest of Jerusalem a knight named Hugh of Payens proposed setting up a body of knights specifically to protect pilgrims coming to the Holy City and on Christmas day 1119 nine knights met in the Church of the Holy Sepulchre and took vows of poverty, chastity and obedience. This small but dedicated group gave themselves the name of 'The Poor Fellow-Soldiers of Jesus Christ.' In time the poor fellow soldiers grew into one of the most prosperous and powerful organisations in Christendom. The knights lived in the al-Aqsa mosque on Temple Mount and so became the Knights Templar.

Within a very few years the Templars had made a name for themselves as doughty warriors and achieved an astonishing position of privilege. They had tax exemption and after 1139 owed feudal duty to nobody except the Pope himself. Royalty asked their advice and borrowed their money with the Temple in Paris soon rising to a major financial centre: so much for the vow of poverty. Not surprisingly, this formation of what became a powerful and secretive organisation with its own private army created jealousy and suspicion.

Early in the fourteenth century King Philip the Fair of France suggested that the Templars should merge with the Hospitallers, another order of knights. The leader of this august and powerful body would be no other than ... Philip the Fair of France and after he died, his son would take control. Not surprisingly the Templars rejected his kind offer but the fair Philip was not finished yet. In the middle ages, if one wished to seriously hurt somebody's reputation, one accused them of witchcraft or heresy, or both. In 1307 that is exactly what King Philip did with the Templars. The Royal forces arrested all the Templars they could find and subjected them to the hideous tortures that Mediaeval Europe had perfected. In unbelievable agony, the knights eventually confessed – or apparently confessed – to a whole raft of things from homosexuality to denying Christ and worshiping Baphomet. There has been speculation that Baphomet could be some demon, but perhaps the name is only a corruption of Mohammed.

With the legal case so convincingly proved, Philip approached the Pope and suggested that every Templar should be arrested and in 1312 the Knights Templar were dissolved. The church was not without mercy for the Templars who confessed and offered repentance were pardoned; those that later denied their confessions were burned at the stake.

So much for the international background; how about Scotland?

Perhaps the Templars vanished quietly according to law, but there are stories that they did nothing of the kind. There are legends that the Templars and their treasure simply ducked under the radar. These legends are supplemented by a number of conspiracy theories that the Templars had a store of secrets that ranged from black magic to the real meaning behind Solomon's Temple. When the hierarchy of the Templars was arrested and their organisation broken up, their secrets were carried to an unknown destination and there hidden away. Like the story of Captain Kidd's buried loot, the stories are persistent and based on very slim evidence indeed.

It seems that a Templar sergeants named John of Chalons let slip that before the hierarchy was arrested they sent eighteen galleys of treasure away to an unknown destination. At that time Scotland was waging a very bitter war with England so a less secure destination for a treasure fleet would be hard to imagine, but there are much later claims that the fleet landed in Mull. There are also wild suggestions that the Templars found sanctuary with King Robert 1, fought at Bannockburn and hid their treasure in Rosslyn. Unfortunately for the theorists, by 1312 King Robert had a plethora of veteran commanders who were well used to defeating the English in battle, so had no need for Templar reinforcements, Rosslyn was not yet built and English chroniclers of Bannockburn make no mention of Templars being present – and they would have snatched at any straw to explain their defeat. Apparently the legend grew from a tale that the English looked like winning the battle until another force joined the Scots and turned the tide of battle.

According to more realistic accounts the Scots were winning so the camp followers joined in: they were the 'other force.'

Now to go back a couple of centuries: King David I wanted to be the very epitome of a mediaeval king. He was the son of Malcolm Canmore and Saint Margaret, so with a multi-lingual Gaelic father and a Hungarian-Saxon mother, it was perhaps understandable that he adopted the fashionable Norman feudal system that was sweeping through Europe. He had abbeys built all across the Borders, brought in Norman knights and invited the Templars to Scotland, giving them land in various places. One of these places, and the Templar headquarters in Scotland, was Temple in Midlothian about eight miles from Rosslyn.

Mention of Rosslyn brings back the Sinclair family of the far north. According to legend - and it is only legend - the Sinclairs were connected to the Templars and Rosslyn was built following the lines of Solomon's Temple. The legend states that Catherine St Clair married Hugh de Payens, who later travelled to Scotland on a European trip to raise money for the Templars. This Catherine is a bit of a mystery woman with no real evidence that she ever existed. There is a lot more garbled pseudo-history that talks of the Sinclairs sailing across the Atlantic before Columbus, and tales of Templar graves in Rosslyn as well as unsubstantiated tales of a secret message in the chapel's symbolism.

Dan Brown's *Da Vinci Code* is a work of fiction –albeit a very successful work of fiction that has raised many questions – but long before the book was written there were a number of strange tales around the Roslin area.

The first is set in the chapel itself. One of the most impressive pieces of carving is the Apprentice Pillar, which was said to have been carved by a young apprentice to the Master Mason. While the Master journeyed to Rome, the apprentice continued the work himself, making so perfect a job of it that the Master was jealous and killed the young man on the spot. One carving within the chapel depicts a youth with a gash on his head, which conveniently is said to be the murdered apprentice. It may also be one of the carvings damaged by the rampaging Protestant mob – or one of Cromwell's cavalrymen.

Another legend, or combination of legends, connects Rosslyn with the supposed Templar treasure, although rather than gold or silver, this fable claims that the chapel is the hiding place of both the Holy Grail and a piece of the Holy Rood, the cross on which Christ was crucified. The actual chapel is said to be a copy of Solomon's Temple, rebuilt in Scotland.

Of course such a place must harbour ghosts. The apprentice is said to be here still, as well as phantom monks in black or grey who have been seen both inside and outside the chapel. One interesting sighting was of a monk at an altar with four knights around him. Another legend claims that when one of the Sinclair descendants dies, the chapel is lit up as if by unearthly fire. That story did not come in the wake of the *Da Vinci Code*, but was mentioned by a much earlier author, Sir Walter Scott in his *Lay of the Last Minstrel*. Apparently unusual lights have indeed been seen here.

Although the chapel has held the world's interest in recent years, there is also a significant castle nearby. Roslin Castle is not nearly as well known as the chapel, and is not open to the public, but even to view it from outside gives a glance at one of the most impressively sited castles in the south of Scotland. It sits on a rocky promontory above the North Esk River, only eight miles from Edinburgh but so secluded that it could be in a different world. Come along early on a November morning with the autumn mist drifting through the stark trees and you will be transported to a different time. Come in the spring when the leaves are bright and primroses speck the slopes and listen for the strains of music and the laughter of the young people to whom this castle was home and the men and women who worked in the fruit gardens and orchard that stretched from the castle to the chapel. Apparently the strawberries were famous!

This was another Sinclair property, with the river bubbling on three sides and a drawbridge crossing the fifty- five feet deep gorge that William St Clair of Rosslyn hacked through the rock ledge. He wanted security for his castle and he got it. For all its beauty there is no doubt that this was also a military fortress and it needed to be for the foundation of the castle apparently stretch to the twelfth century and the present building to 1304 when this area was fought over by Scots and English. Only the previous year there was a vicious battle fought at Roslin.

This castle, like all in Scotland, was no Hollywood image but a place of defence. It was attacked during the Wars of the Rough Wooing when Henry VIII of England tried to force the Scots to accept his infant son as husband of the equally childish Mary of Scots by destroying the infrastructure of Scotland and massacring the people. Not surprisingly, he failed but Roslin Castle was only one building that felt the results of Henry's maniacal foreign policy. The St Clair family went to work to successfully repair and improve, so that Mary, Queen of Scots stayed here in 1563 but the following century Cromwell's General Monck left his mark when he pulverised the mediaeval walls with seventeenth century cannon.

The St Clairs – or Sinclairs – continued to live here until the Rosslyn line died out in 1778 although it is heartening to know that the present owners are descendants of the original family.

Naturally all this historic activity has left its mark in the world of the paranormal.

There are at least three ghosts associated with Roslin Castle. One is a white lady. Apparently she was a maid who was attending the children in the castle when a mouse frightened her. She dropped her candle, which started a fire that killed her. Now her ghost, dressed in white and carrying a candle, haunts the castle.

The second ghost is a black knight, who rides a black horse across the bridge leading to the castle, but there does not seem to be a story attached; he is a very mysterious ghost. Given that there was a major battle fought nearby in February 1302, it is possible there was a connection. The third ghost has a much more interesting legend.

During the Scottish victory at the battle of Roslin in February 1302, there was a fight between an English and a Scottish knight. The Scot won, but was immediately attacked by the Englishman's great wolf hound. The Scotsman dispatched the dog, but later that night the hound was heard, baying, around the castle. The phantom dog returned night after night until it was the turn of his master's killer to go on duty. He was walking along one of the passages when the other members of the garrison heard him scream, and then there was the sound of a huge dog. The knight fled through the stone corridors of the castle, and died in an upper chamber. Even today, on stormy winter nights, the hound, once known to the castle garrison as the Mauthe Dog, is heard baying through the woods that surround the castle. If the Hound of the Baskervilles comes to mind, remember that Conan Doyle was an Edinburgh man and probably knew the Roslin story well.

There is another story, not quite ghostly but certainly unusual, that says if anybody stands on one of the stone steps inside the castle and blows a trumpet, a great treasure will be revealed. That story may be interwoven with the legend of the sleeping lady who is also somewhere within the walls of this castle. According to the legend, when she one day wakes she will show some lucky person to a huge treasure that is buried in the vaults. Perhaps the trumpet call will waken her? Another stranger version tells of a phantom white lady who guards a treasure, but she is not free, for sorcery and the spirit of darkness hold her captive.

That story bleeds into yet another curious legend. It is said that in 1834 a certain Count Polli came to the castle from Italy. According to the story he was descended from the last Provost of Rosslyn Chapel, who had been chased away by a Protestant mob. Apparently this sixteenth century Provost took the time to write directions to what were real treasures, the chapel's accumulated books and manuscripts which had been hidden in the nearby castle. Count Polli was said to have recovered many of the books and took them back to Italy with him.

There is a possibility that this story is confused with the supposed Templar treasure of nearby Rosslyn Chapel.

Although Roslin takes the crown of the unusual in Midlothian, there is a plethora of unusual activity in the area. For instance nearby

Gladhouse Reservoir is haunted by the ghosts of a couple who were murdered while they were courting. To the west is the twenty mile long range of the Pentland Hills, where there is another ghost. Her name is Morag Mackintosh and she apparently fell in love with one of the French prisoners-of-war who were held in Penicuik during the Napoleonic war. When her father refused permission for her to marry, she killed herself at Lover's Loup, a well known spot in the hills.

As a full stop to the tales around Roslin, in 2009 builders were repairing a ruinous wall beside the old church at Temple when they unearthed what they believe to be the top of a sarcophagus. When the stone was dated, it was found to be from the twelfth century, which would tie in with the Templar foundations of the church. However the symbols carved on the stone are not Templar and nor can they be deciphered. Instead they may be Norse or West Highland, many miles from Midlothian. But Sinclair was from Caithness, at that time under Norse control... Midlothian may only be a stone's throw from Edinburgh, but its mysteries are as deep as any in the country.

Bluidy Tam

He had many nicknames, which is never a good thing. To some he was 'The Muscovy De'il', to others 'Lang Tam Dalyell' or 'Muscovy Tam' but most knew him as 'Bluidy Tam.' General Thomas Dalyell has received a black press over the years, yet he was possibly one of the most loyal men in a period when loyalty was hard to retain; and a professional soldier at a time when the Scottish Army was not at its best.

Dalyell was a Royalist during the great civil war that tore the four nations of the British Isles apart from 1639 until the early 1650s. He played a full part in the Scottish Wars, and when he heard that Cromwell's regime had executed Charles I he is said to have sworn a solemn oath never to shave his beard. After that Dalyell stood out in any crowd, particularly as he grew older. By the time the second Charles ascended the throne, Dalyell was a tall, slender man with a bald head and a long grey beard that stretched below his belt. Unlike his contemporaries, Bluidy Tam refused to wear a wig, and the beaver hat he sported had a narrow brim. With this strange headgear above his beard, and a tight jockey's coat beneath, Dalyell was a distinctive figure as he stalked the streets and hills of Scotland.

According to his contemporary, Captain John Creighton, when Dalyell travelled to London to speak to the king, hordes of cheering boys followed him, but rather than chasing them away, he thanked them for their attention. The king, however, was less pleased by these crowds of unwashed and unruly subjects and wondered why Dalyell did not shave and dress 'like other Christians.'

There were those in Scotland who would dispute that Dalyell was any sort of Christian. His reputation went far deeper than any eccentricity of clothing to forms of cruelty and oppression that ground into the still-emerging Church of Scotland so that his name became a byword for unease in the South West of the country.

Religion and power were at the heart of the troubles that beset seventeenth century Scotland. There was a struggle to control the Church and a dispute about what type of Church there should be. While the power of the Roman Catholic Church was mainly removed from Scotland in the sixteenth century, now the various factions of Protestantism squabbled amongst themselves. There is no need to go into the petty splits and factions, but the main argument was about control. While the Episcopalians sought a Church with pyramidical hierarchy headed by the King and containing a structure of rank including bishops and archbishops, the Presbyterians looked for a democratic church where people were responsible for their own souls.

The king, naturally, disliked to see control of the Church slip away from his hands and so began the religious wars of the seventeenth century. They were as bitter and cruel as any other civil war, and as a Royalist, Tam Dalyell was in the thick of them. When King Charles I was executed, Dalyell was imprisoned in the Tower of London but he escaped to serve Tsar Alexis Mikhailovich of Russia, the father of Peter the Great. For ten years Dalyell fought in the Tsar's army. According to his enemies, it was there that he learned new tricks of cruelty and torture that he brought back to Scotland when Charles II ascended the throne. His name 'The Muscovy Devil' came from these rumours and half truths. In part, this nickname is a gentle play on words, as Dalyell is often pronounced Dee-il or Deil, the same as the old Scots name for the devil.

In truth Dalyell was the antithesis of the more extreme Presbyterians, the Covenanters who took to the hills of the South West during the years of their persecution. While they were reputed to be humourless and sombre, devoted to psalms and the Conventicles, the religious gatherings among the hills with only the sky for a roof and pewits for music, Dalyell was anything but. It was during these bad, killing times that Dalyell earned his reputation. He was a pleasure loving man with a mistress in Russia and perhaps a couple more in Scotland, with whom he sired a brood of children. He liked cards and gambling, drinking, roistering and boisterous parties that any other gallant cavalier would have envied, so he was seen as ungodly and unchristian by the grim Covenanters. When he returned from Russia, Dalyell brought with him a reputation for ruthless efficiency edged with cruelty, and the Covenanters wasted no opportunity to blacken his name.

Forgetting their own behaviour in the aftermath of the Battle of Philliphaugh, when they happily drowned the wives, children and camp followers of the Royalist army, the Covenanters accused Dalyell of every imaginable sin. According to them, he was a tyrant and a devil worshipper. He had sold his soul to Satan. He consorted with demons. He played terrible games in his house of the Binns. He tortured prisoners and hanged men at their own front doors.

The list is formidably shocking, and some of the accusations may even have a vestige of truth in them. As a battle-hardened soldier who had experienced war fighting for the Tsar against the Poles, Dalyell had undoubtedly witnessed some terrible things; it is unlikely he treated the Covenanters, lineal descendants of the men who had committed regicide on his king, with gentle sympathy.

As Commander in Chief of the King's Army in Scotland, Tam Dalyell was responsible for ending the Covenanters insurrection of 1666. More commonly known as the Pentland Rising, this little war involved some hundreds of Presbyterians engaged in a spirited but hopeless march from the South West toward Edinburgh in an attempt to ask the king to redress their grievances. In atrocious weather, Dalyell marched the two thousand or so soldiers of the Scottish Army across the country; met the Covenanters in the Pentland Hills and in a bloody little encounter that showed the stalwart heroism of the Presbyterians, won his battle. Fifty Covenanters were killed, and about one hundred and thirty killed in this Battle of Rullion Green.

The aftermath was not pretty as first the Royal troops murdered thirty of the camp followers and prisoners and then Dalyell stuffed his prisoners into Haddock's Hole, an exposed part of Edinburgh's Greyfriars Kirk. From there many were transported as bonded slaves to the Americas and others hanged at Edinburgh's Mercat Cross. Dalyell continued to press hard on the Covenanters, allegedly using thumbscrews and an atrociously repulsive torture instrument called the Boot to learn the names and whereabouts of other Presbyterians.

Although the thumbscrews had been known in Scotland since around the fifteenth century, Dalyell was slandered with the dubious honour of having introduced them from Russia. While that device for crushing the thumbs was an awful enough instrument, the Boot was truly chilling. Simple in construction, the Boot was a box that fitted around the shin and, when wedges were hammered in, crushed the bone so the marrow eased through. Dalyell was not blamed for inventing this monstrosity; he was only accused of agreeing to its use.

Probably more effective in preventing any real threat of revolution were the Scots Greys. This regiment of dragoons – the name came from the 'dragon' or type of firearm the original dragoons carried- wore grey cloth that Dalyell ordered specially after seeing the camouflaged Polish cavalry. These grey horsemen became expert in hunting down the Conventicles and harrying the hill-preachers that roamed the damp green hills of the Presbyterian west. And Dalyell was blamed for that too.

In the 1680s the persecution hit a new high as the Killing Times peaked. There had been another insurrection in 1679, with the twin battles of Drumclog and Bothwell Brig seeing the Covenanters hopes rise and then shatter. In 1680 the Covenanter Reverent Donald Cargill summarily excommunicated Dalyell and Charles II for:

killing pillaging, robbing and oppressing... the Lord's people and free subjects of this kingdom... for this lewd and impious life leading adulteries and incleanness from his youth

This was a time of hatred and rumours, of women tied to stakes and drowned in the rising tide of Solway, of soldiers billeted in the homes of recalcitrant Presbyterians, of hidden Conventicles in the hills, of Episcopalian ministers stripped and abused by bands of screaming Covenanting woman, of sordid beatings and tragic families watching their men hanged, of women cast into pits filled with snakes and spiders and masked hill-preachers rallying the extremists.

Outside the turbulence of South West Scotland came the Rye House Plot, an attempt to depose Charles II, whose tentacles spread across England and deep into Scotland. The idea had been to kidnap or kill both the king and his son, the Duke of York as they travelled from Newmarket to the mansion of Rye House. A fire had caused Newmarket to be evacuated early so the timing was upset and the plot failed. Many prominent Scottish Covenanters were implicated, including an excommunicated minister called William Spence who was tortured by sleep deprivation, the Boot and what the Council minutes blandly described as: 'the use of a new invention and engine called the thumbikins which will be very effective.'

Dalyell supervised the interrogation, along with George, 'bloody' Mackenzie, a judge who had sentenced many Covenanters to the gallows or slavery in the Americas. Just two years later, in August 1685, General Thomas Dalyell died. It was said he was admiring the painted ceiling of his town house in the splendidly named Black Jack's Close in the Burgh of the Canongate beside Edinburgh. Marion Abercrombie, his fourth wife, was said to be quite upset. It was fitting that he should have a glass in his hand, and more than fitting he had a military funeral. He was seventy years old.

The funeral was a solemn occasion. His own Scots Greys were there, as well as the Scots Guards and six pieces of artillery; his baton was placed carefully on top of his coffin and his boots were hung, reversed, from his saddle as hundreds gathered to watch him go, or perhaps to ensure that he was finally dead. Leaving the Capital by the Portsburgh, the funeral procession trundled westward to Abercorn Church, not far from Dalyell's seat in The Binns in what is now West Lothian. Old Tam of Muscovy, Bloody Tam, was dead and a generation of Covenanters breathed their relief.

But although the body of one of the last of the Cavaliers and possibly the most loyal of the Royalists was dead, his spirit lived on. The Binns began to resonate with rumours. There was the legend that Dalyell and the Devil used to regularly play cards. Not unnaturally, the supernatural powers of the Devil ensured he won most of the games, but on one occasion he lost and was so frustrated he lifted the heavy marble card table and threw it out of the window. Hundreds of years later workmen were employed in the grounds outside the Binns. When they drained the Sergeant's Pool, where the Scots Greys had once watered their horses, they were astonished to find the same table as deposited by the devil. For years before this event, this pool was said to be the home of a water spirit that dragged people to their death.

It might have been after this card game that Dalyell and the Devil argued, and the Devil threatened to blow The Binns down. Shortly afterward, Dalyell added the towers that firmly nail down each corner of the building. They are still there, and so far the Devil has not blasted down the Binns.

Dalyell's third son Jon had taken charge of the boots and took them home to his own home in Fife, but night after night they kept the house awake by marching around, so John returned them to The Binns. It was also said that if cold water would boil if they were poured inside them.

Dalyell himself has also been seen riding through the Black Lodge and onto the grounds of The Binns. His horse is pure white as it gallops over the Errack Burn carrying Dalyell along the old, now seldom-used road. Strangely, another spirit was also said to infest this entrance to the grounds.

Today The Binns is a quiet spot although the legends remain. Few people know about the Battle of Rullion Green in the Pentlands, but Greyfriars Churchyard still has a strange atmosphere; and the mausoleum of Bloody Mackenzie glowers at the space where his mortal enemies, the Covenanters, had once suffered and prayed. Dalyell's memory survives, although the cause for which he fought has long passed.

However, Lang Tam was not the only Royalist to enjoy a black reputation. When Sir Archibald Kennedy of Culzean died, the devil was seen in the midst of a storm, carrying away his corpse. The Duke of Queensberry was another disliked man and when he died his soul was transported into a black coach drawn by six black horses. The coach took off from Scotland at great speed and rattled to Mount Vesuvius where a voice roared out: 'Open to the Duke of Drumlanrig!'

True or not, such legends show the depth of feeling against those who persecuted the Covenanters.

Curse of the Egyptian Bone

There have been many films and books about the mummies of Egypt. Some have been good, some have been less good. Some have centred on the idea of a curse invoked after opening the tomb of a mummy. Perhaps this is only fair, as for centuries western nations have been plundering the tombs of Egypt as if by right, and western archaeologists and adventurers have carried many fine Egyptian treasures far from their homeland.

However, although Scottish museums hold their share of Egyptian artefacts, there is only one strange Scottish tale of Egypt striking back, but that was in Edinburgh, surely one of the most haunted cities in the world.

Edinburgh's Dean Bridge crosses a fascinating chasm, with the Water of Leith surging over a weir below and the swaying trees of a private garden adding colour. It is a lovely part of Edinburgh, particularly in the soft just-before-dawn light when birdsong sweetens the air and the day's work has not yet begun. The Dean Bridge connects the bustle of Princes Street with a select area of Georgian and Victorian houses, and it was in one of these, in Learmonth Gardens, that Scotland met Egypt. In 1936 Sir Alexander Hay Seton, 10th Baronet Seton had been on holiday in Egypt with his wife Zeyla. He had been impressed by the temple at Luxor, but less so by the Valley of Kings. Only the tomb of Tutankhamen had been worth visiting, he thought. However when an

Egyptian guide offered to show them a recently opened 'pre-Mummy' tomb, behind the Great Pyramid, he and Zeyla had come along.

Speaking about the event later, Sir Alexander said he 'had a feeling in my bones that something was going to happen over this and it was only with the greatest of difficulty that Zeyla cajoled me into going.'

They descended a few steps to a rock-hewn tomb to view a 'four or five thousand year old' skeleton of a female; he reckoned it was a princess. While Sir Alexander disappeared for a smoke, Zeyla returned for a last look. She returned with a small, not particularly impressive piece of bone 'rather like a digestive biscuit' in Sir Alexander's words and she thought that was souvenir enough from her trip.

The irony of this story was, although Sir Alexander Hay Seton believed that the curse eventually settled on him, it was his wife Zeyla, who had actually taken the bone. Sir Alexander placed the object in a small glass case on a table in his dining room as an interesting talking point and invited friends for dinner. As the party was ending, part of the roof parapet broke away and came crashing down, missing the Hay Setons by only a few feet. With the Learmonth Gardens houses being of solid, quality construction, there was no explanation but at that time it was passed off as an unpleasant coincidence.

It was only a few nights later that the nanny complained of noises in the drawing room, but when Sir Alexander checked he found nothing. However there was a downpour outside and perhaps the rattling of rain on the windows in those pre-double-glazing days had alarmed the nervous lady. The next morning the small table was overturned, the glass case was on the floor and the bone lay at its side; Sir Alexander blamed his own carelessness and the vibration of passing traffic. The small incidents continued: footfalls on the stairs when there was nobody there, unfamiliar sounds throughout the night time house and a pattern of broken sleep. Even worse, a young nephew staying in the house claimed to have seen a ghost: a female dressed in unfamiliar, foreign clothing.

After a time, Sir Alexander decided there must be a burglar after his valuable antique snuff boxes and stayed up to stand watch. Locking the drawing room door, he remained on the balcony outside his bedroom, watching for intruders and waiting to see what transpired. After a few hours of utter silent boredom, he returned to bed and was sleeping when his wife's screams woke him up. There was another disturbance in the drawing room, and when he grabbed his revolver, fumbled for the drawing room key and burst in, he found the place in a complete mess, with the chairs scattered all across the floor and the books from the bookcase thrown everywhere. The bone was there too, outside its case and looking, he said, 'more like a biscuit than ever.'

A visit to a local 'soothsayer' cost £1 for no help at all, but when the drawing room continued to be disturbed Zeyla thought that the bone may be the cause of all the upset. They moved all the furniture, including the bone, downstairs to the sitting room and for a while there was peace, but one night the room was turned upside down and the bone was sitting happily amidst the turmoil.

To Sir Alexander, the solution was obvious: destroy the bone and end the disturbances, but Zeyla did not agree and told him so, forcibly. It was her bone, after all, she was his wife and he kindly allowed her to have her will. The story leaked to the press, and a journalist borrowed the bone for a week before returning it. Sir Alexander half –hinted that the journalist later had a car accident, and that may be true, but in the meantime the drawing room was again disturbed and the table on which the bone stood was damaged.

The next incident was possibly the worst so far. Sir Alexander and Zeyla had argued; she had gone to her family and he to his club, leaving the nanny alone in the house. She heard some terrible noises and when Sir Alexander investigated he found the table was broken, the glass case smashed to pieces and the bone itself broken into 'about five pieces.'

Now Sir Alexander invited the press, but the journalist who covered the story became dangerously ill: the bone came back to Learmonth Gardens and the unsettling happenings continued. Zeyla had a doctor repair the bone and learned it was a sacrum, from the base of the spine, and once again it was placed on a table in the drawing room.

Sir Alexander held a Boxing Day dinner party with a large and boisterous group invited and a roaring fire to keep the drawing room warm. Naturally the guests had heard about the famous bone, and it became a topic of conversation, much to Sir Alexander's dismay, for he had heard quite enough about it, thank you very much. In this case Sir Alexander did not have much to say, for the bone itself proved the star of the show. As if it was aware it was being discussed, the bone jumped from its position, taking the table with it, and crashed against the far wall of the room. Not surprisingly, there was consternation, with one of the maids and one of the female guests fainting. The party continued downstairs, with the bone left well alone.

The story was now well known, and newspapers in America as well as in Scotland published accounts, not all accurate, about the famous Egyptian Bone. Spiritualist meetings were held and even Howard Carter, who had uncovered the tomb of Tutankhamen, wrote a private letter to Sir Alexander.

Despite his wife's wishes, Sir Alexander decided that the bone had to go. Fighting ancient curses with Christianity, he invited Father Benedict of Fort Augustus Abbey, who happened to be his uncle, to exorcise the bone, which was then thoroughly burned.

That seemed to be that. There were no more instances of flying chairs or moving books, but Sir Alexander was certain the curse remained as his life was dogged by misfortune. His daughter Egidia needed an ear operation, as did Zeyla; he had trouble with his own health, and within three years his eleven year marriage to Zeyla ended. His second marriage lasted nearly twenty years before also ending in divorce and on the event of his third marriage he predicted his own death within six months. He was dead within the year.

Did the Egyptian bone carry a curse? Or was there just a series of coincidences and a perfectly normal, if unsettling poltergeist. It is very unlikely if the truth will ever be known.

The Phantom Armies of Scotland

Perhaps it is because of its centuries-long history of survival against overwhelming odds, but Scotland has a proud military tradition that is nowhere more obvious than in the capital. Edinburgh is dominated by its castle with the annual military tattoo and statues of William Wallace, King Robert I and Earl Haig to mention only three. However Edinburgh is not unique; other towns and cities also have their military monuments. William Wallace guards Stirling and Aberdeen, while Inverness has the splendid Fort George a few miles to the east and everywhere, from remote Strathnaver in the far North West to the wary towns of the Borders, there are memorials to famous regiments of or honoured dead.

Given this background, it is hardly surprising that phantom armies should also march across this land, or appear in the hazed void of the sky. During the last three hundred years, ghostly armies have been witnessed in many locations throughout the nation, sometimes by reputable observers; at others by women and men unsure quite what they saw.

One of the most interesting examples was in the 1720s when General Wade's men were constructing the engineered roads that were intended to keep the Highland clans under control. Much of the actual construction was undertaken by local Highlanders, so when they dug up an ancient stone cist they guessed exactly what it was, and who it contained; they did not wish to disturb the incumbent. However, with natural curiosity, the redcoats that worked alongside them prised open the cist and looked inside. A massive skeleton glared blankly up at them.

'It's Fionn,' declared the Highlanders, 'or Ossian,' and they explained as best they could that the skeleton belonged to one of the ancient Gaelic heroes from the days before time. The Fionn were tall men, near giants who had defeated all their enemies, and these were the bones of a huge ancient hero. At first the redcoats were inclined to scoff, but the engineer in charge ordered that the bones be left where they were until he had definite orders, and he sent a message to General Wade. The General told them not to touch anything until he saw for himself, but before he arrived, the cist and skeleton had disappeared.

When Wade made enquiries, the Highlanders looked blank: they did not know what had happened. Nor did the redcoats, at first, but gradually a strange story emerged. Some of the sentries, watchful in case of Jacobites or cattle thieves had seen something completely different. One soldier had seen a long column of men, each carrying a lighted torch through the dim of the Highland summer night. As they marched the men were chanting, a constant, uncanny sound that raised the hackles on the back on the sentry's throat. These men had carried the cist away.

Since that night back in the 1720s, the stone cist has never been seen and nobody knows where the bones of the ancient hero lie, or who carried them away. Perhaps, like King Arthur or King James IV, Fionn is hidden beneath a sacred hill, waiting until Scotland is in mortal peril before rising from their grave to save the nation.

There was another, far better documented sighting of a phantom army only a few years before, when in January 1719 Alexander Jaffray, Laird of Kingswells, was riding with a friend a few miles to the west of Aberdeen. Both were educated, level headed men, and both saw a phantom army in front of them. It was no fleeting glimpse from the corner of an eye, but a fully fledged uniformed army of some seven thousand men, complete with a commander on a white horse and the colours of each individual battalion. The day was bright, crisp and clear and the two men watched the army manoeuvre to its drummers for a full two hours. Eventually the army marched away, to vanish behind a hill.

There was no explanation for this army, and no reasons for it to return in October of that same year, again with the drummers and the commander on his white horse, but this time there was firing, with smoke jetting from the muskets, but no sound of gunfire. 1719 was a traumatic year in Scotland, with a Jacobite Rising and a small Spanish army landing on the West Coast, but the resulting battle in Glen Shiel had no relation to the phantom armies witnessed on these occasions. Nonetheless, some people visiting Glen Shiel have reported seeing men fighting with swords and muskets, which could refer to the battle of 1719.

Sometimes, however, the armies may not even be military. There is a spectral force that marches silently beside the River Ness and quietly enters the High Kirk of Inverness. They are silent men who do not carry arms and there is no explanation for their presence. Some have speculated that these are the dead from the battlefield of Culloden, but they might be just people from the town. Only one thing is certain: only a few are blessed enough to witness them as they file into the church.

In the eighteenth century, as Scotland came to terms with her new position as northern partner in a supposedly equal union with England, Inveraray in Argyll was a hot spot for ghostly armies. On the 10th of July 1758 five different witnesses, in two different places, watched a battle take place in the skies above the town. They saw a Highland army, complete with kilts and bagpipes, assault a French army behind powerful fortifications. Although the Highlanders charged repeatedly, they were thrown back and defeated. Strangely, while the image floated in the sky, there was a real battle taking place in North America as the Black Watch charged the French garrison of Ticonderoga and lost heavily. This part of Argyll also has a squad of redcoated soldiers marching along the A819, although they have not been seen since houses were built on the area. These soldiers were reputed to be English, but could be of any of the nationalities who made up the British Army of the eighteenth century.

Only a short distance away and a handful of years after, in 1765, a father hid his son from an entire regiment of redcoated soldiers in Glen Shira. Red coated soldiers had a bad reputation for brutality and violence in eighteenth century Scotland. The soldiers in Glen Shira were marching in formation and, as they were accompanied by their wives, children, camp followers and baggage; they were obviously engaged in a serious move. When the father looked up to make sure the road was safe, the regiment had vanished completely, leaving no trace of its ghostly passage.

The eighteenth century was a time of warfare in Europe. Until the Union, Scotland as a nation was hardly involved in European warfare, but in that century there was barely a decade when Scottish soldiers were not marching and fighting in some European dynastic squabble. That might explain why there were so many sightings of phantom armies in the country. Early in 1774 a man named Stricket saw a lone phantom horseman, and later that year he saw an entire army marching in silence. He watched it for a good two hours before it vanished, and there were no other witnesses.

Of all the hundreds of battlefields in Scotland, perhaps none is more evocative than Culloden, a few miles outside Inverness. It was there, on the bleak Moor of Drumossie, that Prince Charles Stuart's mainly Highland Jacobite army was outnumbered, outgunned and slaughtered by the highly professional force of the Duke of Cumberland. This can still be an uncanny place, especially around the anniversary of the battle on the 16th April. For those who have the power to see and hear, the spectres of the dead return on that date, together with the clatter of weapons and harsh slogans of the clans. Sometimes men are seen sliding though the grave mounds and murmuring in Gaelic to themselves. It is said that birds do not sing above the grave mounds where the clansmen, killed in battle or murdered in the bloody aftermath, were laid to rest.

One particular ghost is said to be tall and slender, with a gaunt face. Legend says he repeats the word 'defeated' which seems a little unlikely as the majority of the Highlanders would speak only Gaelic. There are other stories: in August 1936 a women from Edinburgh was at the moor when she saw a swathe of tartan across one of the grave mounds. For some reason she removed the cloth and there underneath was the body of a dead highland warrior – or so the story goes.

Culloden also has St Mary's Well nearby, where the spectres of dead Highlanders are said to congregate. Legend says that the Hanoverian soldiers dropped the bodies of the Highland dead and perhaps still dying here after the battle. One persistent tale also recounts the tale of the so-called Great Scree. Apparently the night before the battle Lord George Murray, one of the leading Jacobite commanders, saw a large black bird hovering over the future battlefield. It is said that anybody who sees this bird will have bad luck.

Added to this, around the turn of the nineteenth and twentieth century the entire battle has been seen again by at least one witness.

The battles of the Jacobite Risings seem to have some sort of power to return, for people have also witnessed the Battle of Killiecrankie. This encounter took place in 1689, when the country was split in deciding which particular dynasty should occupy the palaces and thrones of the United Kingdom. Although the parliament in Edinburgh had chosen William of Orange as the next king, there were many who preferred the more direct Stuart line and wanted James VII to return. Bonnie Dundee, Graham of Claverhouse, led the mainly Highland army that marched south to dispute the succession, and just north of the Pass of Killiecrankie in Perthshire he faced the Government Army of General Mackay.

The battle was short and decisive. Dundee's Highlanders swept aside the redcoats in a single bloody charge and chased the survivors all across the countryside, but Dundee himself was killed, some say with a silver bullet. Some people have seen this battle re-fought on the

27th July, with the ferocious Highlanders sweeping down the tangled hillside and the redcoats firing a single volley before they broke and ran. The ground is said to turn red with blood.

One incident that deserves to be recorded happened in a summer evening in 1513 in Edinburgh. A local man named Richard Lawson was walking up the High Street to get to his home when he heard trumpets blaring around the Mercat Cross. He stopped in amazement when something red, like blood, eased along the ground and a strange creature with horns like a goat appeared. Was that the devil itself?

As Lawson stared, the creature announced that within a few months there would be a terrible battle with many dead. It began to proclaim the name of all who would die, beginning with his Grace, King James IV. The list seemed endless, with aristocrats, nobility, chiefs and finally the ordinary men. When the creature shouted out the name Richard Lawson, its sole audience stood in shock for only a second. As soon as he recovered his senses, Lawson sunk to his knees and prayed to God, then, pulling a coin from his purse, he threw it at the creature. The coin was a silver goat with a Christian Cross on the reverse. The power of the Cross worked; the creature burst into flame and disappeared.

Obviously shocked, Lawson ran to the king and gabbled out what he had seen. However King James took no heed and within a few weeks he led a Scottish army to defeat and slaughter at the Battle of Flodden. While King James and a huge number of his men were killed, Lawson was one of the survivors. He returned to Edinburgh with news of the defeat.

There are questions of course. Was the story actually told before the battle, or fabricated after? And there were rumours that King James wife Margaret had paid an actor to be the creature in an attempt to stop the impending war.

Not all the armies are of such recent date. Not far from Forfar in Angus is the site of the Battle of Nechtansmere, where the Picts defeated a formidable Northumbrian Army and reclaimed this part of what is now Scotland from Anglian rule. This battle was fought in 685 AD, but there are still resonances. As well as the small Standing Stone in the village of Dunnichen, men in Dark Age clothing have been seen searching the corpses that lay strewn over the ground.

Nechtansmere was fought in the seventh century, but even before then, professional soldiers marched across the then-untamed glens and hills of the country. The iron legions of Rome had conquered half the known world, but they faltered in two or three places. The equally powerful Parthian Empire matched them man for man and sword for sword; the Germans ambushed them in the dense forests, and the Caledonians fought them to a standstill. The Romans built two walls to mark their British frontier; Hadrian's Wall in Northern England and Antonine's Wall across the narrow waist of Scotland. Probably the most important Roman camp in the part of Scotland that they temporarily held was that of Newstead, beneath the triple peaks of the mystical Eildon Hills. And that is where they have left some sort of ghostly presence, for just occasionally people have reported hearing the measured tread of marching feet on this outpost that some thought might be forever Rome.

It is not hard to find reminders of Scotland's martial past. Every city, town and village has its memorial to the dead of the First and Second World Wars, with lists of men who often outnumber the present population as a stark reminder of the blood price. There are literally hundreds of battle and skirmish sites throughout the country, most unmarked, where Scots fought invading English or Norse, clan fought clan or Scot fought Scot in sordid squabbles over dynasty or religion. The ghost armies, seldom seen, are only echoes of these bad old days. Hopefully some time humanity can see how stupid war is and instead spend the billions currently wasted on war and weapons in the pursuit of peace and medical advances. Until that day, there is always the possibility of more phantom armies being seen from future, unimaginable wars.

Requium for the Unionist Duke

It was 1707. To many people in Scotland, that year was horror enough, as those in power, either through bribes or threats or self-interest signed their names to a paper that merged the Scottish Parliament with that of England and Wales. The ensuing riots and protests showed exactly what the majority of the Scottish people thought of this betrayal of their nationality. However, those who signed the Articles of Union patted their inflated pockets and returned home well satisfied with their thirty pieces of silver.

Of all the Scottish Commissioners who supported the Act of Union, the Duke of Queensberry was perhaps the most extreme. Known as the Unionist Duke, he never varied in his support until long after the sordid deed, and a favourite pastime of the Edinburgh mob was to stone his coach when it rumbled through the city. Nevertheless, however rosy things were politically and financially for Queensberry, he also had family troubles. He had a son, the Earl of Drumlanrig, who was known as a monster. Today the Earl would probably be cared for in a well-run establishment, but back in the early eighteenth century there were no such places. Instead Drumlanrig was securely locked away in a room in Queensberry House at the foot of the Canongate, only half a mile from the Scottish Parliament that his father had so effectively betrayed.

But that morning of January 16th 1707, the Union Duke was away and it seemed that in the excitement nobody had bothered to feed

Drumlanrig. Either his door was insecure, or the Earl was very strong, for he escaped from his room and began a search for something to eat. He seems to have roamed the rooms for a while, and eventually made his way down to the kitchens, where the food should be. Unfortunately, the first person he met was a kitchen boy, a young boy whose principal duty was to turn the spit on which would be thrust the meat.

To the disordered mind of Drumlanrig, the solution was obvious. He was hungry; he had seen how the kitchen spit system worked, and here was a ready source of food. It is unknown if he killed the young boy before he impaled him on the spit, but when the Unionist Duke returned home flushed with success and bribes, he found his son calmly eating the roasted remains of the kitchen boy. It was perhaps a fitting requiem for the day's work.

An Heir for Iain The Toothless

Most Scottish clans have a vibrant and often bloody history, but that of the MacLeans of the Island of Mull is perhaps more bloody than most. They have a history of splintered loyalties and inter family feuding that caused great hardship and grief at the time, but which has left a legacy of some fine stories. Few more so than that of Iain the Toothless, Iain Maclaine of Lochbuie, who surely had one of the strangest sequences of events even of a Hebridean chieftain.

To begin with Iain Maclaine of Lochbuie had a family dispute with his own son, Eachuin of the Little Head, who envied him his lands and position. The arguing turned to violence and then into a full scale feud. In 1538 there seems to have been a battle and one of Iain's followers beheaded Eachuin with a sweep of his claymore.

Now Eachuin's headless ghost can still be seen around Lochbuie Castle, a portent of death for one of the MacLaines. That little matter left Iain the Toothless as undisputed head of his branch of the MacLeans, but also left him without a son and heir. His major rival for power in Mull was Hector MacLean of Duart Castle who was a tougher enemy than Eachuin had proved. The focus of the story now switches to Hector. He had to go softly or he would precipitate another feud that might weaken him when Clan Donald and the Campbells were always waiting their chance for a land grab. So rather than kill Iain the Toothless outright, Hector MacLean kidnapped him and carried his rival chief to the tiny island of Cairnburg and left him to languish there. There is nothing on Cairnburg except a grim castle and the endless surge of the sea.

Hector MacLean knew that once Iain the Toothless died, his lands would accrue to Duart, unless there was another heir. Accordingly, Hector searched for the ugliest possible woman to act as maidservant and shipped her over to Cairnburg. Judging by his name, Iain the Toothless was no great beauty himself, and either his idea of feminine charm differed to that of Hector, or enforced abstinence made him desperate but when MacLean sent a man to check on Iain, the maidservant was heavily pregnant.

Infuriated that his plan had fallen apart, Hector sent a boat to Cairnburg and grabbed the woman. Bringing her back to Mull, he placed under strict guard and hard orders. If the woman had a daughter, then well and good and the direct Lochbuie line was broken forever, but if she had a son, then the baby was to be killed outright. A midwife remained with the woman when her time was near, and when the child appeared it was a daughter. Immediately the baby came, the midwife ran to inform Hector MacLean. When the midwife returned to the house, she was stricken to find that the woman had given birth to a second child, a boy that was given the name of Murdoch.

The baby had already been hidden away and although Hector MacLean ordered a search, he could not find it. Eventually Hector learned that Murdoch had been taken to a cave in the wild area of Beinn Fhada, and he sent his caterans to find and kill the MacLaine heir. Hector MacLean rounded up all the people who lived in the area, including a father and three sons, who happened to be the unofficial guardians of Murdoch. One by one, Hector asked the three sons where the MacLaine heir was hidden, and one by one the sons denied all knowledge. As their father watched, Hector killed the sons, also one by one.

Lastly, Hector put the same question to the father and he was proud when he gave the same answer, adding that he would die thankfully as none of his sons had betrayed their trust. Then Hector killed him too. A later generation of Gaels would suffer similar persecution for their loyalty to a Stuart prince. This casual murder is marked by the place name Arinasliseag: the 'place of the slashing.'

Murdoch was not located. He grew up safely and was known as Murdoch the Stunted, but with Mull being so dangerous he had to leave. At that time the Gaeltachd extended all across the Highlands and much of Ireland, so he moved to Gaelic Ulster, where he would be welcomed. Years later he returned with a dozen experienced fighting men, with whom he challenged for his position as chieftain. Recruiting local MacLaines who had retained their loyalty to the old line, Murdoch and his dozen captured Moy Castle, and Murdoch the Stunted eventually became the chieftain of the MacLaines of Loichbuie.

It was a tale of loyalty and faith but also of treachery and bloodshed and slaughter that shows something of the darker side behind the bright image of tartan and screaming bagpipes. However romantic the backdrop of grey stone castles and mist shielded mountains, the chiefs were as capable of treachery and murder as any other robber baron anywhere in the world.

Sawney Bean

Sawney Bean is the cannibal per excellence. When anybody mentions Scottish cannibals, it is Sawney Bean who springs to mind and no wonder. His is a story of horror, murder and cannibalism that would be suitable for any late-night Halloween film.

Sawney or Alexander Bean was supposedly born in what is now East Lothian, not far from Edinburgh, sometime in the sixteenth century or perhaps earlier: legends tend to concentrate on the gist of the story rather than specific details such as times and dates. Sawney's father was apparently a ditch digger and hedger, which was a hard job that did not appeal to the son a great deal. He tried for a while but soon looked for something easier than labouring to earn his daily bread. He found a wife, or at least a woman, and together they left home and wandered across Scotland for a while until they reached Bennane Head in Carrick, in what is now North Ayrshire.

Rather than live conventionally, Sawney and his wife found a deep, secluded cave in the coast, possibly Bennane Cave itself, 200 yards long and with the entrance blocked by the sea at high tide. Here they settled, about half way between the town of Girvan and the village of Ballantrae, and from here they began to make the country hideous for locals and travellers. The main coast road passed close by, and people began to disappear, at first individually and then, as the years passed, in pairs and even quite large parties.

At first there was not much notice taken of the odd disappearance, for travel in mediaeval or even Renaissance Europe was never safe, with footpads, outlaws and robbers joining the natural hazards of flood, shockingly poor roads and fickle weather, but in time people noticed a pattern. They realised that travellers in the south west seemed very prone to disappear and they began to wonder why. Local people became very wary, but despite their caution, they could not work out what was happening.

In the meantime, Sawney and Mrs Bean had been busy. Perhaps the honest toil of ditching was not to their liking, but there were other occupations in which they excelled. As the years passed, they produced eight sons and six daughters and then eighteen grandsons and fourteen granddaughters. Indeed, they seemed to breed prolifically, if incestuously for all the children and grandchildren had only themselves for partners, and as soon as they were old enough, the young Beans played their part in this family business.

Some people are born into a culture of cannibalism and know no better; others have it thrust upon them from necessity and starvation, but Sawney Bean and his wife took to it from choice and proved themselves experts.

With the cave a virtually perfect hideaway, they rarely ventured out in daylight but prowled the roads by night, using their growing clan of predatory monsters to ambush any lone traveller. As the Bean clan grew, they became bolder, tackling larger and larger groups. Once the Beans murdered their victims, they carried the bodies back to their cave, stripped them, cut them up and ate whatever they most fancied.

Whatever was not immediately eaten they would pickle, presumably in sea water, of which they had an unlimited supply, and the inedible portions were simply thrown into the sea for the tide to distribute wherever it pleased. Perhaps it was the reappearance of these bits and pieces of unfortunate humanity that alerted and alarmed the local folk into taking more direct action. Gathering together, they began to search the area, poking into every nook and cranny, eyeing any stranger with great suspicion and hanging the odd unfortunate who happened to be a little eccentric in their ways.

They even looked at Bennane Cave, but when they saw the tide wash right inside they thought that nobody could live there. And still the murders and cannibalism continued as Sawney Bean and his clan bred and thrived and preyed on everybody into whom they could sink their blood stained teeth. Over the period of time in which the Beans operated, they must have killed scores, perhaps hundreds of people, so Sawney might have felt virtually invulnerable as he continued to be undiscovered. Yet everybody's luck has a way of levelling out and one night the Beans overreached themselves. There was a fair held a few miles away and they left their cave and slithered through the dark countryside, gathering in a hideous ambush to await any unwary fair goer.

Given their lifestyle they must have been a terrible sight: they would be unwashed and ungroomed, stinking of dried blood, with long talons for nails and eyes more akin to predatory animals than a family of human beings. Their ears, tuned to hunting, would hear the sound of approaching people before they were seen, and then two people rode happily into view. They were obviously man and wife, both sharing the same horse on their return from the fair and more intent on each other's company than in watching for any possible cannibal ambush. When the pair was fairly within the circle of Beans, the cannibals attacked.

It must have been a terrifying experience for the pair; one second they were happily riding, laughing and reminiscing, the next they were surrounded by dozens of screaming monsters with grasping claws and gaping mouths. However, that part of the Scottish West Coast is Kennedy country, and in the sixteenth century Kennedy men were well able to take care of themselves. This man was no peasant farmer with only a stave, but a gentleman with sword and pistol and the verve and skill to use both well. Firing, slashing and stabbing, he beat off the first attack, but as he tried to ride through, his wife slipped from the back of the horse and before the husband could turn, a group of female Beans had ripped out her intestines and were gorging themselves on her blood even as her horrified husband watched.

The fight had reached its climax; the husband would be staring unbelievingly at his wife, but then a second group of people returning from the fair appeared and the Beans vanished into the sinister dark.

It was too late for the wife, but now people knew that there was a whole clan of cannibals infesting the coast of Carrick and they sent news to the king. James VI has had a bad press from historians, and often with reason. He was a callous man who tried to pacify his Gaelic speaking subjects by forcing a foreign culture on to them, a weak man and anything but brave. However, he was also a king who gave Scotland decades of peace and when the occasion came, he quietened the riding clans of the Border with some skill and sufficient ruthlessness to ensure the old wild system did not return. Now he acted with speed and decision.

Although some accounts claim the king came in person, it is much more likely he ordered the local lords to sort things out. Either way, a small army of four hundred men scoured North Ayrshire, but this time they were accompanied by hounds. The dogs followed the trail of blood and the four hundred men formed up around the tide-swept Bennane Cave. The army moved in; the Beans fought back but they were outnumbered and overpowered. Tied hand and foot, they lay in sullen fury, glaring at the invaders through vicious, only semi-human eyes, and only then the invaders lifted their torches and examined their surroundings.

At first they could hardly believe what they saw. The whole cave, some hundreds of feet long, was festooned with human remains. There were chunks of human flesh hanging to dry, legs and arms pickling nicely in barrels and glittering piles of silver coins, watches and whatever else could be gleaned from the bodies of the dead. Overall was the stench of cooked human flesh. Rather than just execute the Beans out of hand, the army placed them in chains and dragged them to Edinburgh, where they were thrown in the Tolbooth, Scott's *Heart of Midlothian*. Normally the Beans would face trial, but the evidence was overwhelming and the King ordered them removed as quickly as possible.

Legend says they were taken to Leith, possibly where the old Gallows stood half way down what is now Leith Walk, or perhaps on the Sands, and executed. The men were castrated, had their hands and feet hacked off and were left to bleed to death. The women had the pleasure of witnessing the death of their men, and then were burned to death. According to one nineteenth century version of the tale, none of the Beans gave any sign of that repentance that the Victorians demanded, but died cursing their executioners.

There is a supporting legend in the small fishing port and holiday town of Girvan, where they claim a women of Bean's clan had already left the cave and settled there. She is said to have planted the locally famous Hairy Tree, but when the townsfolk discovered who she was, they hanged her from the tree she had planted.

If Sawney Bean had spawned an entire clan of cannibals including grandchildren, he must have been rampant in Ayrshire for at least twenty years and probably more. Yet there does not seem to have been any contemporary evidence to support his story. It was not until the publication of sundry chapsheets in the eighteenth century, followed by the *Newgate Calendar* in the early nineteenth century that his story became widely known, which tends to raise suspicions as to its truth. Some of the supporting facts are also suspect: Sawney's occupation of a hedger and ditcher seems unlikely in a sixteenth century Scotland where East Lothian was virtually denuded of trees, yet alone managed hedges. The method of execution was also unheard of: even witches were strangled before they were burned and castration was not a Scottish method of punishment. Lastly the Hairy Tree must have been extremely fast growing to mature enough to bear the weight of the woman who had planted it.

However, it is possible that the legend had endured from an earlier period and contemporary story tellers merely added details to suit the susceptibilities of their audience; a retelling in the manner of *Apocalypse Now* for *Heart of Darkness*.

But it is easy to feel safe and sceptical and superior so far away in time and distance. Perhaps it would be an idea to visit Bennane Cave some dark November night when the tide is turning, and venture to the back of the darkness, wait, and listen for the sounds of crunching bones and watch for the predatory, evil eyes.

Between the Sexes

In Scotland, as in other countries, men and women came together for companionship, sex, love and marriage. Sometimes they got along very well, and on other occasions things did not go so well.

For example there was the chief of the MacFarlanes whose marriage was not all it could have been. His wife was a wayward, unfaithful woman and strayed from MacFarlane toward the neighbouring chief of the Colquhouns. Not only did she seduce him, but she did so in the bed she shared with her husband, and it was here that he caught them both.

Naturally MacFarlane was angry; he drew his dirk and threatened the Colquhoun, who jumped out of the bed, deserted his lover and fled naked from the house. MacFarlane's wife did not scream: she was unfaithful but still the wife of a chief. Instead she waited for her husband's anger and his revenge. He did nothing; he did not even raise his voice.

For the next few weeks, MacFarlane treated his wife with more affection than usual, if anything. A few days later he even insisted on making her a meal, and then served the food himself. Noticing that the MacFarlane was watching her closely, the wife asked why, and he motioned to the dish that had just been served. Curious, she lifted the lid and screamed in horror. MacFarlane's men had killed Colquhoun, and he had castrated the body and now served the genitals to his unfaithful wife.

However, not only clan chiefs, but also women often had a way of retaliating. Highland women in particular could extract singular vengeance. In the Middle Ages Lord Walter Comyn, one of the Comyns of Ruthven Castle in Badenoch, decided to amuse himself by forcing the youngest and most attractive of his tenant women to work naked as they collected the harvest. He appointed a certain day for this amusement, and rode over the hills from Atholl especially to view the splendid sight.

The day arrived and the young women unclothed themselves and huddled in the fields, with their older sisters and mothers repelling any local man who hoped to capitalise on the warped humour of their lord. However, time passed and there was no sign of Lord Walter, so that his retainers grew worried. Sending out a search party, they scoured the hill passes, until a horse bounded toward Ruthven Castle. It was Lord Walter's horse, but was obviously terrified, with foam flecking its flanks and its eyes rolling in its head. What was worse, one of Lord Walter's boots was trailing from the stirrup, with a piece of his leg still inside.

Sick with worry, the searchers redoubled their efforts until, at the rocky gorge of Leum na Feine, the Fingalian's Leap, where the River Tromie thunders into the Spey, they found what remained of their lord. His body was lying shattered on the ground, with two eagles feasting on his eyes and entrails. Of course, the local women knew exactly what had happened: Lord Walter had died by witchcraft and the eagles were two of the women whose daughters he had forced to work naked in the fields.

There is a similar story in Glen Lyon in Perthshire, where the Stone of the Demon marks the spot where Governor MacNab of Carnban Castle broke his neck in a fall from his horse. According to local legend, an enraged mother had cursed MacNab after he forced girls to work naked in the fields.

Highland women seemed particularly expert at this laying of curses when their offspring were threatened. The Clan Mackintosh had its Curse of Moy, where the Chief of Clan Chattan ordered a young man to be hanged for sheep stealing. Naturally upset, the man's mother begged for mercy, but the chief refused. The chief had the power of pit and gallows, imprisonment and death and the man was a thief. However, the mother was vengeful and had power of her own.

If you take my son from me, then I shall take the son of Mackintosh from him. From this day forth the chieftainship of Clan Chattan shall never descend from father to son.

It is said that the curse was effective.

The catalogue of shame and horror is long, but there were one or two gleams of humanity. At the end of the Eighteenth century Alexander, the 23rd Chisholm chief, perhaps persuaded by his wife and daughter Mary resisted every attempt to evict any of his tenants in Strathglass. After his death in 1793, his widow and daughter continued to protect the people. On one occasion a lawyer tried to force his ageing widow to sign an eviction notice, but Mary threw him out with threats and high words. As a counterpoint to the Duchess of Sutherland, Mary Chisholm should be better remembered, as should the brave women who faced the muskets and truncheons of authority with stones and their own bodies.

Christie Cleek the Perth Cannibal

While Sawney Bean, the Galloway Cannibal, is famous even outside Scotland, few people have heard of Christie Cleek, yet his existence is more probably fact than legend. Despite the passage of time, quite a lot is known about this predatory man. His name was Andrew Christie, he came from St Johnstown of Perth and he was a flesher, which is the old and very appropriate Scots name for a butcher. Nobody knows how long Christie Cleek terrorised the good people of Perthshire and the southern Highlands, but his name is mentioned in the chronicles of the time, so he made an impact on the nation even at a time of massive troubles.

Christie Cleek lived during the mid fourteenth century, which was a grim time for Scotland. With the death of King Robert I in 1329 the English revoked their promise of perpetual peace and once again attempted to conquer Scotland. The armoured chivalry of England, reinforced by those Scots who hoped to benefit from supporting the enemy, invaded the nation, and again the Scottish people endured slaughter, murder, looting and devastation. Naturally the Scots did not tamely bow down before the invaders so that armies marched and countermarched and the land was marred by battle, siege and ambush, skirmish and atrocity. Men such as Sir Andrew Moray, William Douglas of Liddesdale and women such as Black Agnes of Dunbar gradually removed the English from the country but it was a painful process.

Constricted by sheer numbers from facing the English armies in open combat except in a few notable cases, the Scots used guerrilla tactics, wasting their own land in the face of the English, denying them food and shelter, even burning the homes of the people so the invaders had nowhere to rest. These burned earth tactics worked, but the Scots paid a high price for freedom from foreign domination.

In the midst of all this mayhem was a downturn in the weather and both combined to create famine. Hector Boece, the mediaeval chronicler who flourished in the period, mentioned floods and plagues of mice and rats, which would make things worse, and people survived as best they could. Either during a siege of Perth or shortly after, Andrew Christie left the town and joined a small band of survivors who had taken to the foothills of the Grampians and lived off the land. Scottish history is full of such incidents, with even such heroes as Wallace living wild for a time: it seems natural. However, Christie did not follow a traditional path. While others might have lived off berries, fish and the wild animals that were much more plentiful then than now, Christie began to hunt for human flesh.

It seemed that when one member of his band died, Christie employed his flesher skills to cut up the body to feed his companions. Whether they knew that they were eating a fellow human or not is not recorded: nor is whether they cared. After eating one man, they had crossed the barrier and began to hunt for more. They infested the passes in the hills and, using a cleek - a hook on a stick - they hauled travellers from their horses, killed them and ate both man and horse. According to Andrew of Wyntoun, who wrote in the 1420s, the gang 'set up traps' for 'children and women for to slay' and 'ate them all that he get might,' so they preyed on the weaker and more vulnerable members of society. Or perhaps women and children had softer and tastier flesh. Other versions of the tale claim that they preferred to kill horsemen, because then the horse could also be eaten.

In time Christie Cleek and his gang came to the attention of the good people of Perth. They sent out a strong party that hunted for the gang and came across the cave from which they operated. The avengers attacked the cave in the evening and there was a bloody fight before most of the cannibals were captured. Presumably they were later hanged, but Andrew Christie, however, is said to have escaped. By that time the worst of the famine must have been over and the English expelled from the country, so he allegedly slipped back into society, and lived a normal life.

A much later addition to the story mentions a merchant in Dumfries named David Maxwell, who lived a prosperous life, married and brought up a family. Apparently he claimed that his brother had been killed by the notorious Christie Cleek, and he frightened his three daughters into obedience by saying that Christie Cleek would get them. Only on his death bed did he admit that everything he said was untrue and he was the infamous Christie Cleek himself.

Perhaps then, there are Maxwells from Dumfries who are descended from this unhappy man?

Major Weir The Wizard

Overlooking the teeming thoroughfare of the High Street with its scores of attendant closes and wynds, Edinburgh Castle should dominate the city, but such is the nature of the burghers that they refuse to bow to even such grim authority. They may appear quieter than the inhabitants of other Scottish cities, just as the cityscape appears more serene, but there is always a hidden side to the Edinburgh character that refuses to conform. It is this duality that has created authors such as Robert Louis Stevenson, and characters such as the thief who was also Deacon Brodie; a mixture of good and evil; people whom it is often impossible to fully understand. Of them all, few can be more oxymoronic than the wizard-gudeman of Major Thomas Weir.

Thomas Weir was one of the most respectable people of Edinburgh at a time when respectability was essential. He was prominent in the 1650s and 1660s, when Scotland was a staunchly religious nation and conformity was not only expected, but demanded. With his long black cloak swirling around him and his blackthorn staff tap-tap-tapping on the gritty Edinburgh streets, Major Weir was a kenspeckle figure in the Capital. He lived at the head of the West Bow, a narrow street that wound steeply down from the High Street to the broad and bustling Grassmarket, and attended every religious sermon expected.

Thomas Weir was a Covenanter, a member of that utterly devout and even extreme sect who founded the Church of Scotland and kept it alive even under the most extreme persecution by the Crown and the Episcopalians. Yet that was not enough; he was also one of the leading lights in the even more extreme group known as the 'Bowhead Saints' – people who would keep an eye on the Lord to make sure he was behaving himself and would brook no nonsense even from other Covenanters.

He did not live alone: Thomas Weir lived with his sister, who may have been called Grizel or possibly Jean, a lady who shared his extreme views and was every bit as devoted a churchgoer. When either of the Weirs appeared, the good neighbours of Edinburgh minded their manners and looked to their Bibles. Not only was Major Weir a churchman, he was also a major in the Town Guard. He was no milk-and water soldier, but had taken his part in the Great Civil War that brought destruction and calamity to the country from 1639 until the mid 1650s, and erupted in minor fashion in 1666. It was Major Weir who commanded the escort that led the great Marquis of Montrose to his execution, and he became the commander of the Edinburgh Town Guard.

In this position he was responsible for keeping law and order within the capital, as well as ensuring the security of the burgh. So as well as spiritual power, he had the authority to order incarceration, fines or whatever retribution he thought fit for any moral or legal backsliding.

Yet one evening, when he led the sermon in his church, things changed. Rather than exhort the congregation to repent for the sinners they undoubtedly were, he began to confess to crimes that were frankly shocking. The congregation listened in stunned disbelief, for they had possibly never heard of some of things to which Weir was confessing.

Scotland being Scotland, and Edinburgh being the city it was, there was an opposite for everything: for every act of genuine piety there was an act of cruelty; for every fragment of Christian charity there was a counterbalance of witchcraft or persecution, and it seemed that Major Weir had being playing both sides. He confessed that as well as a Christian he was a Satanist and a witch; what was probably worse to the outwardly douce neighbours of Edinburgh was that he also said he committed incest with his sister. But as his listeners recoiled in disgust,

Weir continued adding sin on sin and horror on horror. He was also guilty of bestiality, having carnal relations with a number of animals as well as sundry women other than his sister.

There are two reactions to such a list from a celebrity: the listeners either act shocked and pretend to disbelieve, or they enjoy the scandal and watch the downfall of a man who pretended superiority. Weir's congregation was no different to those who read the gossip pages of newspapers today: some thought he had gone mad, others craved more details. Quite naturally, Grizel Weir was hauled in and closely questioned.

She added even more damning admissions, claiming that their mother was a witch who had passed on her magical powers. Her brother, Grizel stated, was a wizard, and the source of his power was the blackthorn staff he carried: that was his magic wand, given to him by the devil himself. The guid neighbours of Edinburgh might have nodded their collective head at that; the marvellous gift of hindsight told them they had wondered at the strange carvings on that strange black staff. Not content with that, Grizel added that the Major had the devil's mark on his body, and had frequently roamed the countryside in a fiery coach, blazing a trail to Dalkeith in Midlothian or to the coast at Musselburgh.

With such an obvious confession from both parties, there could only be one outcome. At that time there was little mercy for witches, and none for an incestuous wizard. Both the Weirs were condemned to death and were hurried down to the boundary where Edinburgh met Leith. Every casual stroller down Leith Walk now passes the old gallows site of this part of Edinburgh, just at the junction with Pilrig Street. In Scotland, witches were 'worrit'- strangled – before they were burned, and before the noose was placed around the Major's neck he was given a chance to redeem himself.

'Will you say "Lord be merciful to me?" ' the hangman asked, but Weir gave another damning reply.

'Leave me alone,' the Major is said to have retorted. 'I will not. I have lived as a beast, and I must die as a beast.'

The hanging duly took place, and when his dead body was burned at the stake, his staff was thrown in beside him. The spectators watched in horror as the blackthorn staff writhed and twisted in the flames, a sure sign it was a witch's wand.

Grizel Weir was also hanged, but she had one final act before her departure. In an age of intense personal modesty, she threw off all her clothes and appeared naked before the shocked neighbours. No doubt they approved as the noose tightened around her neck. It was 1670 and the persecution of witches in Scotland was already beginning to ease off; Major Thomas Weir was said to be the last man executed for witchcraft in Scotland.

However, the Weirs were not yet finished with Edinburgh, despite being dead. The West Bow house in which they lived was shunned for years on account of the strange happenings that were reported there. There was music making and laughter, there was singing and the unmistakable sounds of jollification: sounds that no self-respecting Presbyterian would allow in their house of solemn piety. Sometimes, however, the Major himself would pay a visit, rattling down the steep street in his flaming carriage, and occasionally the staff would appear, travelling by itself as it looks in vain for its erstwhile owner.

In the nineteenth century most of the street was demolished to make way for Victoria Street, but still the ghosts can be heard, and the fiery coach occasionally seen.

The Brahan Seer

Perhaps it is because they lived close to nature, but until fairly recent times, and perhaps ever today, many Highlanders had the gift, or the curse, of Second Sight. Some of these people were only known locally, others had a wider audience and a few obtained a fame that is still spreading.

Among the latter is Coinneach Odhar, or Kenneth Mackenzie, better known as the Brahan Seer. He lived in Easter Ross, around the Black Isle, and his predictions had an uncanny knack of coming true, if not always in the manner imagined by his contemporaries, who could not imagine the world that his visions described.

Although Coinneach Odhar is best known in the east, he was apparently born in the far west, in or near Uig in the Island of Lewis, then, in the dying decades of the seventeenth century, in the possession of the Mackenzies. In many cases, second sight was a family trait, or came because the recipient of the gift was the seventh son, but Coinneach Odhar's case was a bit more dramatic. His mother, who must have also been gifted, was in the habit of witnessing spirits roaming around the local graveyard. Being an enterprising woman, she grabbed one before it returned back to her grave. The spirit protested, but Coinneach's mother refused to let it return until it gave her a gift, and eventually it handed over a small fairly unremarkable stone. Black and blue, it had a hole in the centre, either natural or bored, but either way when this stone was passed on to Coinneach, it gave him the gift of Second Sight that was such a major influence on his life.

From Lewis, Coinneach moved to the shores of Loch Ussie near Strathpeffer on the opposite side of Scotland but still in Seaforth Mackenzie territory. Working on the Brahan Estate, Coinneach began to make prophesies, so in time became known as the Brahan Seer.

Many of the predictions have already come true, many years after his death. One of the most dramatic took place only a few dozen miles from his home by Loch Ussie, when he was walking across the heathery waste of Drumossie Moor. An image or vision of the future came to him and he said:

This bleak wilderness will be stained with the best blood of the Highlands. Glad I am that I will not live to see the day where heads will be lopped off in the heather and no lives spared.

In April 1746, many years after Coinneach's death, two armies squared up to each other across the sodden bogland of Drumossie. While one was nearly ten thousand strong, well fed, well trained, well armed and backed by parks of artillery, the other was much less than half that size, starved, exhausted and bereft of proper training.

For upward of twenty minutes the smaller army stood in line as the larger force battered them with artillery and their commanders dithered, and then they moved forward in the only manoeuvre they knew; the charge. Unfortunately the ground was mostly too soft to get up any speed, the positioning of the rival armies meant different clans had varying distances to cover and they advanced into masses ranks of unshaken regulars. Amazingly, those few score Highlanders who survived the cannonballs, the grapeshot and the volleys of aimed musketry broke the first line of regular redcoat soldiers, but too few remained to even dent the second and they were trapped in crossfire that slaughtered them like sheep.

Culloden was more of a massacre than a battle, but it was the aftermath that still sickens the memory. The wounded were left to suffer and then bayoneted where they lay as Butcher Cumberland began a rule of terror that would make Hitler blanch. The prophesy of Coinneach was proved entirely correct; the best blood of the Highlands stained Drumossie Moor.

It was a direct, if delayed result of that battle that proved another of Coinneach's sayings. He said that the 'clans will become so effeminate as to flee from an army of sheep.' Once again he was entirely correct. After Cumberland's victory at Culloden and the subsequent rape of the Highlands, the British government removed the ancient powers of the Highland chiefs and reduced them to the levels of Lowland or English landlords. Some remained loyal to their people, but others began to view them as a burden, tenants who could not pay their way.

There have been many apologists for the Clearances, and some revisionist historians claim that they were really not so bad, but for the men, women and children who were ordered away from homes their families had occupied for generations, it was a grim, cynical time. For the landlords, either the old clan chiefs or the southern industrialist who bought the land, the people stood in the way of profit. Sheep made more economic sense, so the glens were cleared of their inhabitants to make way for flocks of white sheep.

There was resistance of course. Sometimes the sheep were driven away, at other times men and particularly the women stood and fought with stones and sticks, but the landlord held all the aces. They had the law on their side, and they had the Church, for often the local minister supported the landlord in what was surely one of the most shameful episodes in the history of the Church of Scotland. If neither of these powers worked, the landlord could call up police or military support. And lastly and perhaps most cynically of all, some of the Clearances were carried out when the men were away – either at the fishing, or seasonal harvesting in the south, or fighting in one of the Highland regiments that gave so many men for the country was betrayed them.

The full prediction, however, or at least one version of it, is longer and more complicated. Listening to it today, and wondering at the truths and the yet unfulfilled ramifications, leaves one wondering at the future of the Highlands, and of Scotland itself. Yet, to a Gael like

Coinneach, there was an element of hope stuck in the tail. As this prophesy is still in the process of unravelling, it is worth reading a translation in full:

The day will come when the jaw bone of the big sheep will put the plough on the rafters, when sheep shall become so numerous that the bleating of the one shall be heard by the other from Conchra in Lochalsh to Bun-da-Loch in Kintail. They shall be at their height in price, and henceforth will go back and deteriorate, until they disappear altogether, and be so thoroughly forgotten that a man finding the jaw bone of a sheep in a cairn will not recognise it, or be able to tell what animal it belonged to. The ancient proprietors of the soil shall give way to strange merchant proprietors and the whole Highlands will become one huge deer forest; the whole country will be so utterly desolated that the crow of a cock shall not be heard north of Druim-Uachdair; the people will emigrate to Islands now unknown but which shall yet be discovered in the boundless oceans, after which the deer and other wild animals in the huge wilderness shall be exterminated and drowned by horrid black rains. The people will then return and take undisturbed possession of the lands of their ancestors.

The sequence of events is quite clear, if not a little disturbing. The landowners replaced people with sheep in the late eighteenth and early nineteenth century, and then found that deer forests were popular, so vast tracts of the land became hunting preserves owned by a few. The Gaelic landowners, descendants of the ancient clan chiefs, sold their heritage to pay debts and non-Gaels took over, first English and Lowland Scots and then people from half the countries of the world. The depopulation still continues: vast number of Gaels emigrated to Canada and the United States, and then to Australia and New Zealand: islands not known about in Coinneach's time.

The times of the horrid black rains have not yet come but it is heartening to know they will be followed by the return of the indigenous people to their old lands.

The seer also warned that when it was possible to cross the River Ness dry shod in five places, a terrible disaster would occur. That saying was so well known that when Inverness town council proposed building a fifth bridge in 1937, local people reminded them of Coinneach's prophesy. There were even letters in the press, but the council knew better and built the bridge.

Construction was completed in August 1939 and within weeks Hitler invaded Poland, Britain declared war and Scotland plunged into the six year horror that was the Second World War.

Some of Coinneach's predictions sounded so ludicrous that nobody could have believed them at the time they were made. For example he predicted that when a fifth spire was built in the town of Strathpeffer, a ship would catch its anchor on it. Strathpeffer is a few miles from the sea inland from Dingwall, and Coinneach's words seemed to indicate that there would be a flood of Biblical proportions. It was not surprising then, that some people were wary when Strathpeffer's total of church spires reached five.

The possibility of a flood that could rise to such a level was virtually unthinkable, but the predictions of the Brahan Seer were known to be accurate. And so it proved. In 1932 an airship was at the Strathpeffer games but drifted from its moorings and its anchor chain dragged across Strathpeffer, with the anchor catching on the church spire. Once again Coinneach had been proved correct.

He was right when he spoke of full rigged ships passing Tomnahurich near Inverness too, although few people in his generation could have dreamed of the Caledonian Canal that linked the North Sea with the Atlantic by way of the Great Glen. He was also right when he claimed that Scotland's parliament would return when it was possible to walk dry-shod between England and France. There would be many scoffers at that, as people mistranslated the prophesy to mean Scotland would never again have a real say in running her own affairs, but then came the Channel Tunnel, linking southern England to France and within a few years, the Scottish Parliament opened in Edinburgh.

Perhaps it not a complete parliament yet, but Coinneach probably has another prophesy, not quite understood, to cover total independence.

Many seers are reluctant to reveal their full powers for fear of offending people, and so it proved with Coinneach. Working on the Brahan Estate, the Earl of Seaforth was his landlord and chief, but when he was absent the Earl's wife Lady Isabella fulfilled the same position. The Earl was in Paris on business and Lady Isabella called Coinneach to her and asked what her husband was doing. Coinneach knew, but gave only a half-hearted answer that at once raised Isabella's suspicions. She demanded more and Coinneach, too honest for his own good, told her that the Earl was at that moment kneeling in front of a French lady fairer than she was.

Perhaps it was not the most diplomatic thing to say to a wife who also happened to have virtually unlimited power. There are two versions of what happened next. In one, Lady Isabella handed the seer to the Prior of Fortrose, who condemned him to death for witchcraft, and in the other, Prior Lady Isabella herself ordered Coinneach to be burned alive in a barrel of tar.

He retaliated in the only way he could; by predicting the end of the line of Seaforth:

The line of Seaforth will come to an end in sorrow. I see the last head of his house both deaf and dumb. He will be the father of four fair sons, all of whom he will follow to the tomb. He will live careworn and die mourning, knowing that the honours of his line are to be extinguished forever, that no future chiefs of the Mackenzie line shall bear rule at Brahan or in Kintail.

It seemed a stark, nearly unbelievable prophesy, and for generations it did not happen and the Seaforth Mackenzies continued to command. And then came Francis Humberston Mackenzie. As a child he caught scarlet fever that rendered him deaf and dumb, yet still he found a wife and fathered four children, but they died one by one, leaving him the last of the Seaforth line.

The Brahan Seer is still remembered in the Highlands, and his predictions are still occasionally spoken of. All of Scotland waits for the 'horrid black rains' that will spread such devastation and some await

the return of the Gael to their natural homeland with hopeful antic-
ipation.

The Big Grey Man of Ben Macdhui

Some hills have an atmosphere that is uncanny. They do not always look any different from their neighbour, but any walker with the ability to sense the unusual can catch the feeling that things are not all they should be. The hills around Loch Iorsa in the Island of Arran can be like that; they hold the feeling of unease that may be connected to the old stories of druids that the indigenous population used to know. Sometimes, in certain conditions of slithering mist light drizzle, the Cairn Hills of the Pentlands has the ability to chill, but neither of these places has the silent stalking *thing* that waits on Ben MacDhui.

It is strange that there is no real folklore connected to this hill, no history of druids or human sacrifice or clan battle to create this legend, but perhaps Ben MacDhui does not need it. Perhaps there is horror enough in modern times to bring this big grey man to life, if indeed things from the Otherworld need to be called by events in this.

The late nineteenth century was a fairly busy time in the Scottish hills, with a growing interest in mountaineering among the well-heeled and new routes being pioneered up even the more remote peaks. Professor John Norman Collie who taught chemistry at the University of London, was one of this group of early hill walkers, an experienced traveller who had seen a good part of the world and a scientist who was prone neither to panic nor flights of imagination. Collie had climbed in the Alps, Rockies and Himalayas as well as in Scotland, so he was unlikely to be rattled by any natural phenomenon.

At that period Ben MacDhui was not well known. It is still not a household name on the same level as Schiehallion, Ben Nevis or Ben Lomond, yet at 1309 metres it is the second highest mountain in Scotland. Yet in 1890 it was only a lesser-visited mountain with no reputation, so when the mist closed over Collie as he approached the top his only concern was the weather and the possibility of losing his way. He reached the summit cairn without incident and began the solitary walk back.

Yet after only a few moments he realised he was not quite as solitary as he had believed. He could hear the sound of his own steps, but there was also the sound of something else. He listened, and thought he heard the crunch of somebody else's steps. They had longer spaces than his, as if the walker was much taller than him, with steps he estimated as 'four times the length of my own.'

On that desolate Scottish mountain with the white mist clinging to him and hiding every feature, Collie tried to rationalise his fears. As he related to the Cairngorm Club in 1925, 'I said to myself this is all nonsense...I walked on and the eerie crunch, crunch sounded behind me.'

Experienced traveller and rational scientist or not, Collie was 'seized with terror' and ran down that hill, not stopping for the nearly five miles to Rothiemurchus Forest. As a stiff-upper-lip Victorian he did not admit to his fear until that meeting of the Cairngorm Club, thirty five years later, and only then he said:

'There is something very queer about the top of Ben MacDhui and I will not go back there myself.'

Rather than the ridicule and recrimination he perhaps expected, Collie received support from a number of other climbers who had also experienced strange things on Ben MacDhui. Some spoke of an unaccountable sensation of fear that settled on them near the summit of the hill, and others of seeing something approaching them. This unknown creature was large and dark and sometimes grey, so it became dubbed as *Am Fear Liath Mor*, the Big Grey Man of Ben MacDhui.

There was another learned man, Dr Kellas and his brother Henry who confessed to having seen a giant figure striding toward him on the slopes of the hill. Like Collie, they took the safer path and ran.

As in every case of something out of the ordinary, something that cannot be explained by conventional logic, there are scoffers who seek an explanation within their own ideas of rationality. Some say, quite as if it was a settled answer, that the Big Grey Man is a 'Brocken Spectre', when a low angled sun casts a shadow of the walker on the mist. This phenomenon was first recorded in Germany and may possibly explain one or two of the sightings, but not the huge footsteps that have been heard and seen, or the sinister mutterings, or the occasional actual sighting of the creature that haunts the barren slopes of MacDhui or the unaccountable feeling of dread that settles on intelligent, rational people.

If the people who have witnessed Am Fear Liath Mor were all excitable, impressionable and uneducated, then there may have been some reason to doubt the veracity of their statements, but that is not the case.

Collie was a scientist who had experienced the world and another witness of the Big Grey Man. Alexander Tewnion was also an experienced mountaineer who was on the upper slopes of Ben MacDhui. It was 1943, with the Second World War four years old and Tewnion carried a revolver with him. Once again the mist slithered across the hill, and once again there was the sound of footsteps. Tewnion knew about Collie's experience and began to search for the origin of the sound. He saw a giant shape emerging from the mist and advance quickly toward him and Tewnion produced his revolver and fired three quick shots before fleeing toward Glen Derry.

Wendy Wood the author and patriot also heard something strange on Ben MacDhui when a voice of 'great resonance' sounded across the slopes. She thought it spoke in Gaelic, but the words were unclear. The footsteps sounded a few minutes later. Other people have also heard the whispering Gaelic voice, and others mention a strange humming or whistling. The old time Greenland whalers also mention a strange whistling sound, but it could only be heard at certain times and close to the water. Some call this the 'Singing' and that may well be a better description.

Perhaps the Brocken Spectre could explain the illusion of a giant creature, but the sudden panic that took hold of both Collie and Tewnion is less easy to lightly dismiss. Other walkers have also experienced this sense of terror. The Big Grey Man is seen more often as more people escape to the hills from the pressures and congestion of city life, usually around the Lairg Ghru Pass.

The feeling of unease nearly always comes first, as if the creature has some psychic force that is directed toward these invaders in his territory. Even more alarming, some walkers say they have been compelled toward the vicious thousand foot high cliffs of Lurcher's Crag, as if the Grey Man was driving them over the edge, herding them with fear like a hunter with his prey. The thought is not pleasant. What is even less pleasant is the knowledge that a few, normally rational people, have mentioned having sudden despondency and suicidal thoughts when on Ben MacDhui, as if the Grey Man, or even the hill itself, can drain hope from the walker.

There are some descriptions of this extremely sinister creature. When it stands upright it is over ten feet tall, with long arms; some witnesses have described him as having short brown hair or an olive skin. Most people only realise it is there by the intensity of their sudden fear.

There have also been sightings of giant footsteps, including some from 1965 that shows footprints fourteen inches in length, and a stride of some five feet. That would match Dr Collie's impression very closely, and makes one shudder, if just a little.

There are obvious similarities between the Big Grey Man and giant creatures that haunt other, even wilder areas of the world. The famous Yeti of the Himalayas and the North American Bigfoot are also large and hairy, and some of the people who have witnessed these creatures have also experienced feelings of intense fear. That sensation of fear may not be without a reason and in Scotland may not be limited only to the Cairngorms.

There is the creature 'without a face' that was seen in 1992 by a family holidaying in the very centre of the Island of Arran. It emanated a feeling of great evil. There are other lonely places in Scotland around which the atmosphere can combine with sightings of mysterious creatures. The Cairn Hills in the Pentlands have been mentioned, and perhaps the cairns were significant. Will Grant, the Pentland walker and writer of the 1920s, mentioned that one of these hills was known as Harper Hill, and a harp was the chosen instrument of the druids which gives a link, tentative perhaps, with earlier mystical ceremonies.

Braeraich, not a great distance from Ben MacDhui also has its sinister guardian. In the 1920s Tom Crowley, another man who knew the hills well enough not to be fooled by a twist of nature, saw something terrible on this hill. He described it as huge, grey and mist shrouded, with pointed ears, long legs and talons on its feet. Other people have mentioned a creature on this hill, particularly near Creag-an-aibhse, which is translated roughly as Rock of the Ghost and, like Glen Shee in Arran and the Harpers Hill in the Pentlands, harks back to other legends, sightings or stories of the distant past. The shapeless Braeriach creature is said to shout out and either throw or roll boulders at walkers.

Overall, the Big Grey man and his associated cousins are amongst the most unpleasant supernatural or just plain mysterious, creatures that may be encountered in Scotland. His appearance is almost always accompanied by a feeling of fear, and the assault on the psychology of the walker is akin to a weapon designed to weaken any resistance. Ben MacDhui may be an interesting peak, the second highest in Scotland and a feather in any Munro bagger's cap, but with the Big Grey Man as a guardian, it should be treated with even more caution than other Scottish hills.

Bodies for Doctor Knox

Most major wars bring a period of chaos in their wake: the First World War brought the depression of the Hungry Twenties, Scotland after Flodden was a desperate place and the Wild West teemed with men who had served in one or other of the contending armies of the US Civil War. The 1820s were no different: the last of the French wars finished in 1815, but twenty two years of warfare had taken its toll and a generation had grown up knowing only violence, and many of whom had no knowledge of their father.

Edinburgh in that period was a divided city. On one side was the New Town of elegant terraces and dignified squares, where gentlemen and their ladies rode in coaches and discussed the politics of the day as they overlooked their pleasure gardens. On the other, beyond the muddy ditch that was once the Nor Loch and up the Earthen Mound, was the teeming morass of the Old Town, or the *Auld Toun* in local parlance. Here lived the unfortunates and the poor, crammed into filthy closes and wynds, jammed shoulder to shoulder in tall, unstable tenements, living day to day or hour to hour and always ready to move out en-masse if the occasion demanded. It was Daniel Defoe who said the Edinburgh Mob was the worst in the world, and he had firsthand experience.

It was in this Auld Toun that the monsters lived; two figures that infested the already festering closes off the Grassmarket and preyed on their neighbours and the unwary who sought solace in the reeking taverns and spirit shops that welcomed the scraped pennies of the poor.

Their names have bounced down through time; Burke and Hare, two Irishmen who left the poverty of their native land only to find poverty in their new home. They arrived at a time when Edinburgh was at the cutting edge of medical research, and a certain Dr Knox was one of the leading doctors in Edinburgh.

The medical school in Edinburgh was rightfully famous, and the students required a steady supply of fresh bodies on which to watch and practice dissection. It was normal for bodies of executed criminals to be used, but there were just not enough murderers to go around and so the dissecting doctors gave a Nelsonian blind eye to the origin of the fresh bodies that they paid good hard cash for.

This was the age of the grave robbers, when people crept into graveyards at night time and dug up the most recently buried corpses. That is why many old graveyards have small watchtowers, to watch for the ghouls who struck by night. William Burke and William Hare, however, were not overly inclined to indulge in the hard work of digging before they got their prey; they preferred easier methods.

Burke and Hare had come from Ulster to work on the Union Canal: they were canal navigators or navvies, a breed that had a frightening reputation for violence and lawlessness, so were not perhaps the sort of men a girl would introduce to her maiden aunt. However, a navvy was a working man and a huge step up from a criminal, although the line was sometimes ill to define. They both graduated to Edinburgh and that is where they eventually met.

Burke, an ex-soldier who had travelled a bit in southern Scotland, together with his woman, Helen MacDougal, found lodgings in a somewhat seedy lodging house in Tanner's Close, in the West Port, run by Hare and his woman, Margaret Laird or Logue. Burke already had a wife back in Ireland, but they seem to have had a falling-out and she had remained behind with their children. Hare, who has been described as unbelievably ugly, tended to laugh a lot, while Margaret

Laird was also Irish, a recent widow who seems to have fallen into his arms quite readily. They made a fine foursome.

In that year of 1827 the West Port was one of the lowest parts of a low area, and Burke and Hare were at the bottom end of the scale even there. They fitted perfectly into their environment. At this period, Scotland was an exciting place to live. In the Highlands, whisky smuggling was reaching its peak, and all around the country, people stood guard over the graveyards in fear of grave robbers also known as body snatchers or Resurrection Men who would dig up the newly buried and sell the corpse to a doctor for the purposes of medical research. At one time there was a ready supply of executed criminals who would have been perfect for the purpose but hangings were becoming less frequent in a new atmosphere of leniency, and medical research was blossoming as Edinburgh became one of the leading medical centres of the world. New bodies were always in demand and the fresher the better.

Burke and Hare would be well aware what was happening in their adopted country, but it is unlikely they considered aiding the advancement of medicine until one of Hare's tenants died in his bed without paying what he owed. The old man was called Donald, he was an ex-soldier with a tiny army pension and he owed Hare nearly £4 10/-, which was a considerable sum when a workman was lucky to earn £1 a week. Hare had no intention of losing so much money, so he and Burke decided to sell the body to a doctor. The most prominent was Dr Knox, who taught anatomy at Edinburgh University. His classes were always popular, with scores, perhaps hundreds, of students and others, crowding to watch a recent cadaver being skilfully dissected.

As a pauper, Donald was hardly entitled to a decent funeral, so Burke and Hare bought the cheapest coffin possible, filled it with bark to give some weight and had it solemnly interred; it is unlikely there were many mourners. With that business completed, Burke and Hare took old Donald's body, covered it and thrust it into a cart. Wheeling it through the grimy streets of the Old Town, they chapped on Dr Knox's door, handed over the body and accepted their reward. Obviously Dr

Knox was delighted to have some fresh material with which to work, for he handed over £7 10 shillings and thanked them very much. And if ever any others of their tenants should die suddenly, don't forget where he was...

That was easy money to men who had made pennies by the sweat of their brow and the muscles of their back, so Burke and Hare saw the possibilities. All they needed was a few more deaths and their pocket books would be jingling with silver and gold. Unfortunately, there was no absolute guarantee that their tenants would die during the night so they decided to help the next one along a little. With whisky plentiful in Scotland, Burke and Hare plied their tenant Joseph Miller with enough to stupefy him and then cheerfully suffocated him. Dr Knox asked no questions as he accepted the fresh body, and Burke and Hare were once again in the money.

With profit so easy, the pair began to hunt for fresh victims. Their next was an elderly woman called Abigail Simpson, who was innocent enough to accept their invitation to enter Hare's lodging house, and was efficiently dispatched. Burke, or perhaps Hare, found it better to smother his victims rather than hit them on the head or stab them: that method left no tell tale marks for any suspicious doctor or medical student. In time people referred to this method of murder as 'Burking' and for a while it entered the vernacular language of the people. In fact Burking was so efficient that Dr Knox was impressed by the quality of the body and he paid Burke a stated £10 for the body: two months wages for a labourer.

With the Old Town a happy hunting ground for warm bodies and Dr Knox obviously happy to pay for fresh corpses with no questions asked, Burke and Hare began a murder spree that makes them probably Scotland's most prolific mass murderers of the nineteenth century. The total is said to have come to at least seventeen and perhaps as high as thirty in little more than a year, and the people around the Grassmarket and the Cowgate must have shivered at the unexplained deaths in their midst. Yet the authorities seemed unconcerned; those who vanished were from the bottom end of the social scale and in a time when chimney sweeps could leave boys to die in the cramped flues of houses, and semi-nude girls dragged huge loads of coal through stygian darkness underground, a few gutter dwellers more or less did not matter. However, although there was little interaction between the haves and have-nots of society, there was one level where the two species met, and that was the most intimate.

Prostitutes were an easy target for the murderers. Their job demanded they go with men, they were numerous and often vulnerable, so when Burke invited two to the lodging house, nobody was surprised, although there might have been a few questions as to why his current woman allowed such dalliance. As was not uncommon in the Old Town, there was an argument, and one prostitute, Janet Brown, stormed off, which left Mary Patterson alone. She was Burked, of course, and her body carted over to the ever-willing arms of Dr Knox. The gold changed hands, Mary was whisked off to the dissecting table and next morning a class of medical students gathered to learn the intricacies of the human body.

When the day's corpse was revealed, two or three muttered their surprise, for medical students were no better than they ought to be and some were already quite familiar with the curvaceous intricacies of eighteen-year old Mary Patterson's body. However, people could die quickly in the back closes and a body was only a learning resource. The lesson continued, and so did the Burking. Victims followed each other in a grim procession of betrayal, suffocation, death and dissection, with always the esteemed Dr Knox passing over the gold and the students learning the art of dissection and anatomy across the violated body of the murdered.

There was the beggar Effie, a grateful woman who believed Burke was helping her escape the police and then others, including Ann Dougal who was a relative of Burke's wife. The cold-blooded heartlessness of that shows exactly what kind of people these murderers were.

The killings continued in a flow of smothered bodies, a year of trips across the Edinburgh cobbles pushing a creaking barrow and the quiet chink of gold coins into the Irishmen's grimy hands. Next was a woman named Peggie Haldane who had been searching for her mother Mary, who had also ended in Dr Knox's butcher shop. Like the other Mary before her, Mary Haldane was a weel-kenned woman, but once again Burke and Hare escaped detection, so they and their women could live the easy life. Daft Jamie Wilson joined the growing list; he was also very familiar in Edinburgh, a good-natured lad who ran errands and never seemed to lose his good humour. People would miss Daft Jamie, and wondered at his unexpected death. His mother asked awkward questions and it was said that Dr Knox denied his anatomical subject was Jamie and ensured he was unrecognisable by dissecting the face first. Nevertheless, Burke and Hare's run of luck continued until they argued. Hare accused Burke of murdering people and selling the bodies without giving him a share. After such a professional disagreement it is hardly surprising the partnership dissolved and Burke and McDougal opened their own lodging house. It was in here that Burke murdered an Irish woman named Mary Docherty.

This third Mary was barely dead when two of the tenants returned unexpectedly and found her body lying on a bed. The link to the other murders was too obvious to miss and one lodger, Ann Gray, refused McDougal's offer of silence in return for a huge bribe and ran to the authorities.

Although Burke quickly transported the body to Dr Knox, the second lodger, James Gray, easily identified Mary Docherty and the police made their arrest. For weeks the questions got the authorities nowhere, but then Hare turned King's Evidence and confessed all. Perhaps he was still bitter over the previous dispute, but he revealed chapter and verse over their career, and Burke was also ready to speak. He admitted to murdering sixteen people but also said he had never robbed a grave in his life.

The trial began on the 29th of December 1828, and not surprisingly, the jury found Burke guilty and on the 28th January 1829, he was hanged in the Lawnmarket. A crowd of some 30,000 mustered to see him die, with some urging the executioner to 'Burke him!' Ironically, as an executed murderer, his body was handed over for public dissection in the Edinburgh Medical School. There are also stories of medical students retaining areas of Burke's skin and either keeping them as souvenirs or selling them for profit. His death mask is still on display in Surgeon's Hall, along with his skeleton and a book covered with his skin.

Because he turned King's Evidence, Hare was freed as was his wife. Helen McDougal, Burke's wife, was also released as there was no evidence against her. She tried to return to her house but the blood of the Edinburgh mob was up and they attacked her with volleys of stones so she had to flee, some said to Stirling, others to Australia. She is rumoured to have died in 1868. The crowd also tried to lynch Margaret Laird, but she slithered free and is rumoured to have returned to Ireland. Hare was held for about a month and then released; there are many rumours about his later life. Some tales say he was last seen in Carlisle, others that a mob attacked him and threw him into a lime pit, so he eked out his old age as a blind beggar. Knox continued as a dissecting doctor, buying his corpses until the Anatomy Act of 1832 released a further supply of corpses for medical research. Knox moved to London, worked in the Cancer hospital and lived another thirty three years.

Today Burke and Hare, the Irish navigators who became perhaps Scotland's most prolific mass murderers, are well remembered in Edinburgh. Ghost tours and other underworld experiences feature the pair, but in reality they were only a pair of utterly callous killers with no redeeming features.

Wolf of Badenoch

Even on a bright day, Lochindorb Castle has an aura of menace as it squats around its island, brooding over a past of mayhem, siege and bloody violence. It can only be approached by boat as it sits about half way down the length of Lochindorb, but marginally closer to the eastern shore. The loch itself is not the easiest to access, with an unclassified road winding over the Dava Moor, so Lochindorb Castle, situated just where Highland Region clicks into the neighbouring Moray, remains off most tourist routes, and that may not be a pity. This grim little castle on its bleak island is perhaps not the best advertisement for Scottish tourism: Vlad Dracula, Adolf Hitler and Attila the Hun may have felt at home with the man who made this place his home, but surely few others.

This castle ruins look exactly what they are, the remains of a lair of a robber baron, the unprepossessing, uncompromising, unromantic home of Alexander Stewart, the Wolf of Badenoch. As so often in Scottish history, the greatest villains had royal blood and the Wolf was no exception. Alexander Stewart was the fourth son of King Robert II, hardly the most successful king in Scottish history, but he did manage to sire one of the most interesting characters. Alexander Stewart was a wayward youth who had a spell in the dungeons of Lochleven Castle in 1368 and who lived his life well beyond the fringes of any law, civil, clerical or moral.

While his Gaelic speaking followers would know him as Alasdair Mor Mac an Righ, big Alistair, son of the King, and the Scots speaking would think of him as Alexander Stewart, history has remembered him as the Wolf of Badenoch, one of the baddest of bad men ever to stalk the blood-stained plaid of Scottish history. Murder; rape, rebellion and fire raising were only some of the crimes of which he was guilty, while myth and legend would add child sacrifice, witchcraft and devil worship to the unholy list.

Alexander Stewart was big in many ways. From the 30th March 1371 he was the Lord of Badenoch, that beautiful country of hills and valleys south of Moray and west of the Cairngorm massif, and that same year he leased the lands of Urquhart, to the west of Inverness. Already a powerful man, he expanded further to possess Strathavon and then his royal father made him Lieutenant of the country north of Inverness. When he also had lands in north Perthshire and Aberdeenshire it was obvious that Alexander Stewart was the most important man in northern Scotland, although the MacDonald Lord of the Isles may have disputed that, if their paths had ever crossed. But Alexander was not yet sated; he became the royal Justiciar for the Appin of Dull and then in June 1382 he married Euphemia, the Countess of Ross.

In most marriages of the landed classes, the man would take immediate control, but Scotswomen were notably independent and Euphemia was no exception. She kept her small hands tight-gripped on the fertile lands around Dingwall, the old Norse capital of that part of Scotland, as well as holding Skye and Lewis, the two largest and arguably most important of the Hebrides. However, Alexander's unhappiness at his wife's retention of power did not prevent him from grabbing more, and the king made him Earl of Buchan, so he was a man with true princely possessions. Yet he is remembered more by his nickname and rampaging behaviour than for the lands he controlled.

Perhaps it was his wife's reluctance to relinquish control over her own lands that angered the Wolf, but it is more likely to be her inability to produce a litter of cubs for his lair. He knew he was fertile, for his mistress, Mairead Inghan Eachann gave him children with near monotonous regularity. Perhaps the fair Euphemia's natural displeasure at her husband's behaviour had something to do with her actions: at this distance in time we can only conjecture.

One of the many legends attached to the Wolf claims he packed his wife elsewhere so he could enjoy the favours of Mairead in peace, which may well be true. He is also said to have had forty illegitimate children, which makes one wonder how many descendants he has today. He was, after all, a Stewart and they were a notably sensuous breed. One of his children became the Earl of Mar after abducting the Lady of those lands, but he was also a pirate and a notable warrior who fought MacDonald of the Isles to a standstill, so the Wolf had powerful seed.

So far the Wolf comes across as a womanising, turbulent, grasping sort of landowner, but Scotland was cursed with hundreds of that type, so how does he stand out? It began with his womanising. Big Alexander was already an un-friend of Alexander Burr, the Bishop of Moray. As the Lord of Badenoch, the Wolf had some sort of authority over the church-owned lands in Badenoch, but Bishop Burr was probably most displeased at Big Alexander's rule by sword, fire, fear and the cateran. A cateran was a lightly armed Highlander, a man who could cross miles of moorland to raid steal or murder, depending on what his chief wanted, and when the chief was Big Alexander, the want was usually a combination of all three, with some spoilage or rapine thrown in for good measure. However, back in 1370 Big Alexander had promised to protect the Bishop's lands and men in Badenoch, so he did not anticipate any trouble from that quarter.

So when Euphemia appealed to Bishop Burr for help after being abandoned by Big Alexander, only the Wolf was surprised that the Bishop should wholeheartedly take her side.

It was not a good idea to oppose Alexander Stewart. He was said to rule Badenoch by fire and fear, and there was no doubt that he surrounded himself with a bevy of some of the wildest men in Scotland. The Highland caterans had a fearsome reputation for bloodshed, rapine and violence, and if the stories have worsened in the telling, there is no doubt that the truth was bad enough to chill even the Moravian heart.

The stories claimed that the Wolf had sold his soul to the Devil in some obscure ancient ritual. They claimed that he and his caterans drank blood behind the walls of Lochindorb Castle and he owned a copy of the Book of Black Earth. This book was one of the most terrifying tomes in existence, with spells and dark knowledge dating back to the days of pre history. Alexander Stewart had called together the *chailleachs*, the witches, of the Highlands and had copied the words from their own mouths. The spells were horrible to relate, but included drinking human blood. It was said that the Wolf held court in an ancient stone circle in the Moor of Granish near Kingussie, where he held terrible rituals that included drinking the blood of still born babies.

Even the place was enough to chill the blood of any right-thinking man, for the Moor of Granish was not the sort of place to take your granny for a Sunday afternoon walk. At that period it was home to an amazing collection of standing stones and stone circles, including one of three concentric stone circles. However it may have been the circle on the shores of Loch nan Carrigean where the Wolf held his justice court. It was thought that, once inside these so called 'Druid Circles' evil was powerless, and it was said that the ancient Picts announced their kings here, with appropriate ritual. According to myth and legend, for there seems to be no historical documentation to back up these stories, when one High King of the Picts died, all those hopeful to replace him gathered at the stone circle, together with the chief druids of the nation. The druids called up the spirits, who helped decide who would be the next king. However, it was fatal to look directly at such a spirit, so the druids had to look at the reflection in the loch.

Such stories may or not be true, but in a superstitious age, such things were often related and believed. It is more likely that Alexander Stewart was just a wild, grasping man with more power than sense and a body of savage followers. It has also been suggested that Alexander Burr, the Bishop of Moray started some of the more extreme rumours about him, but in any case, the Wolf left his lair to wreak his own peculiar kind of vengeance on the holy man who had turned against him.

Whistling up his caterans, Alexander Steward left Lochindorb and descended on the fertile lands of Moray. He ransacked the town of Forres and turned on Elgin, the ecclesiastical capital of Moray and the home of the bishop. His caterans ran riot, burning the College, the Canon's houses and the hospital of the Maison Dieu. Unable to stand against these professional fighters, the good people of Elgin fled to the countryside while flames from their town rose in a funeral pyre to the heavens.

Still not satisfied, in 1390 the Wolf burned Elgin Cathedral, the Lantern of the North and one of the most splendid pieces of architecture in Scotland. As well as the structural damage, the Wolf's arson attack also destroyed irreplaceable documents, family records and legal decisions. His attacks were an assault on the bishop and people, but his arson was an affront to history itself.

King Robert ordered his son, the Wolf, to do penance for burning Elgin Cathedral, and came in person to ensure that he obeyed. In front of the king, an assembly of nobles and a collection of church dignitaries, Alexander Stewart rode down to the church of the Blackfriars in Perth and did what was required of him. Perhaps because of his royal blood, or because of his armed power, the Church allowed him back into its grace. However, a wolf cannot change its nature.

Alexander Stewart continued to live at Lochindorb and other castles in Badenoch, and he extended their defences. He did not make any further major raids into Moray but there were as many legends about his death as there were about his life. Even the date is disputed: it may have been as early as 1394 or as late as 1406. The people of Badenoch spoke of his last night, when he stayed in Ruthven Castle. A mysterious man called, clad entirely in black came to call. They began a game of chess, playing for hours, until the tall man in black called out 'checkmate'. As soon as the word was said, a storm began, with thunder, lightning and hail, so that the good folk of Badenoch took shelter. In the morning, all the caterans were dead; lying twisted and blackened as if struck by lightning, while the Wolf's body was in the banqueting hall, with all the nails in his boots removed.

The Wolf was buried two days later, with a freak local storm centring around his coffin as it left Ruthven Castle. He lies today in Dunkeld, a long way south from Lochindorb, and further south still from the gaunt ruins of Elgin cathedral that his men treated so badly. A strange feeling can still be felt on the Granish Moor where the Wolf dispensed his unique brand of justice, and a vague rumour persists, growing weaker year on year, that when real danger threatens Scotland, those who know the secrets can call up the spirits and ask for their help. But there was little help for Moray when the Wolf led his caterans north and perhaps that is why, on a certain day, it is possible to creep to the gaunt remains of Ruthven Barracks, where the castle once stood, and look through the window of time to see the Wolf and his devilish companion playing their eternal game of chess.

There is a small local legend that claims that one day two local lads saw a strange blue light flickering around the ruins. As they investigated, they saw a highland chief and a band of hunters ride down from the hills with a dead deer across the back of a pack-pony. Slipping closer to the castle, they watched through a window as the hunters feasted and drank, as well as following strange rituals that the boys did not understand. After a time, the walls of the castle opened up and a man stepped in. Wearing a long black cloak, a black hat and black gloves, he was tall and slender. Words were spoken and the man in black began to play chess with the chief of the hunters. Literally spellbound, the boys were unable to move as even the moon stayed static in the heavens as the chief and the man in black played. Eventually, after an unknown passage of time, the man in black said:

'Checkmate.'

Immediately the word was said, a tremendous storm of lightning and thunder began, with sleet and hail that battered off the ground. The boys found the spell lifted and ran for their souls. In the morning, shaken but still curious, they returned to find the castle a ruin and the bodies of all the hunters outside, dead, black, twisted and burned. The chief alone remained in his chamber, seemingly uninjured save that all the nails in his boots were missing.

It was a couple of days later that the chief's funeral procession began. The sky darkened and a thunderstorm began, but only around the coffins; the weather was clear all around. The legends of the Wolf of Badenoch remain.

Wicked Lord Soulis

From the high middle ages until the union of the crowns, the border-land between Scotland and England was one of the most fought over regions in Europe. Armies marched and counter marched as national differences were contested by kings and princes, and in the periods of peace, cattle reivers, outlaw bands and various types of wild men created their own brand of mayhem. Of all the valleys of the borderland, Liddesdale was arguably the wildest, and deep in the heart of Liddesdale, Hermitage Castle sat, squat and uncompromising, attempting to keep some form of peace.

It has been called the Cockpit of the Border and the wickedest valley in Britain and both titles could be correct. Beginning just on the border line, a stone's throw from the old Debateable Land, Liddesdale forks north eastward into the long green hills, running at times nearly parallel with the long-disputed frontier with England. And this was a disputed frontier: long before the first boatload of Saxons nosed across the North Sea from Germany, the ancestors of the Picts faced the invading Romans in these damp hills, and their battles set a precedent that was to last for generations after the Union of the Crowns was supposed to pacify the Borders.

Britons fought Romans and their descendants formed petty kingdoms that fought each other as much as they drew swords against the pagan Saxons from the south. King Arthur may well have been here with his Myrddin or Merlin; Old King Cole reigned in Kyle, only a long day's ride to the west, while Wallace and Bruce, the Black Douglas and the Bold Buccleuch knew these hills as well as their own battle scarred castles. And in between there were raids and counter raids, plunder and rapine, reiving and razing of houses. The Borderland was not a place to breed quiet people, and Liddesdale was possibly the most dangerous and violent place in the Borders, so it is no surprise that many of the legends are of wild men and wild deeds.

Liddesdale was home to the reiving clans of Elliot, Nixon, Crosier and Armstrong; men whose allegiance was purely to the head of the riding family, with king and country not worth a snap of their calloused fingers. Before them, when life was, if anything, even more precarious, it had been home to the Wicked Lord Soulis.

While the Borders had been split into Marches - areas under their own Warden - since the early middle ages, Liddesdale was always bad enough to have its own guardian, and he lived in what George MacDonald Fraser called the 'mediaeval nightmare' of Hermitage Castle. There is nothing attractive about this building as it sits beside a sullen peaty burn in a side valley; it has no pretensions to a romantic Hollywood idea of a castle: it is functional, gaunt and grim. Nobody could mistake it for anything but a guard house and garrison, a keeper of the savages of the valley, a police post for violent criminals and an outpost more dangerous than any in the American Wild West.

The castle has ancient roots and was first mentioned around 1240 when Nicholas de Soulis was the owner and keeper. This original castle would probably be timber built, a simple motte and bailey erection to overawe the locals, but it would not be of much use against the siege train of an aggressive king such as Edward Plantagenet of England. In Lord Soulis, Hermitage had a suitably vicious keeper. At the beginning of the fourteenth century the de Soulis lord made himself thoroughly unpopular with the neighbours. At that time Scotland was just emerging from one of the worst periods in her history, the First War of Independence, when the Borders had been particularly badly affected. Yet even so, the people of Liddesdale were concerned when their children began to disappear. They knew at once what was happening: Lord de Soulis was kidnapping them and taking them to the dungeons of Hermitage Castle, where he used them in his diabolical rites. It is possible that de Soulis was a medieval paedophile, using children for his own ends and then disposing of the bodies.

The Borderers had no doubt that he was evil: de Soulis even had his own familiar, a vicious creature called Robin Redcap, an innocuous name enough for a servant of the devil. Unlike most spirits, Redcaps have a specific geographical location; they live only within a score of miles of the Scottish-English border, and inhabit only the ruined castles that are scattered among that area's lovely valleys and bleak uplands. They attack travellers, luring them into the castle and killing them before drinking the human blood to maintain their red cap. In appearance they are small in stature, with long fangs but are very fast moving, and as elementals they have some supernatural powers. Whatever he was, Robin Redcap granted de Soulis a measure of immortality in that he could not be harmed by steel or rope – so he could not be hanged or killed by sword, lance or axe. In return, Robin Redcap demanded blood, blood and more blood, which is why the local children were being abducted. The other name for a Redcap is a powrie and they are not the pleasantest of creatures to emerge from the mists of Scottish folklore.

In time of course, de Soulis graduated from stealing the odd errant child to abducting men and women, but he had chosen the wrong environment. The people of Liddesdale were not the sort to put up with a child- stealing tyrant, no matter how many supposedly supernatural hobgoblins he had at his side, and they resolved to get rid of him. There were two methods of doing this: officially and unofficially. Being Liddesdale men, their first thought would be the direct, unofficial method, but they knew that if they did so, they would offend the king, and he was not of a temper that anybody wanted to offend. King Robert 1 was the victor of a score of battles and his reputation was such that even the men of Liddesdale walked wary of him. Accordingly they approached His Grace with a report of what was happening in the deep south of his country and a request for permission to remove the wicked Lord Soulis from office – and from life.

'Soulis! Soulis! Go and boil him in brew!' King Robert is alleged to have shouted as they made their petition, and if so, it shows an uncanny insight into the problem of killing a man whose devilish familiar had made nearly invulnerable. As they could neither hang him nor use an edged weapon, the people of Liddesdale had to be slightly more inventive in removing de Soulis. It would be no use threatening their Lord with spears or trying to tie him up, so instead they grabbed him and wrapped him in a huge sheet of lead. It was something like a scene from an old horror story, with the local peasants storming the castle and dragging out the Lord. No doubt de Soulis fought back, but he was outnumbered by a people he had made extremely angry.

Confined so he could not struggle or escape, the Liddesdale people dragged him to the Nine Stane Rigg, which is an ancient stone circle on a long ridge above Liddesdale. On this evocative and windy spot, they boiled a cauldron of water and threw him in. It could not have been a pleasant death for de Soulis, surrounded by baying peasants as he slowly boiled to death.

In one version of the legend, the people of Liddesdale drank the 'brew' of boiled Lord Soulis and lead as a sign of triumph and contempt for their defeated enemy, but other versions do not add this colourful detail. It is interesting that the death of de Soulis was given as something like a ritual sacrifice, with the cauldron and the ancient location within a stone circle, which makes one wonder if the story hints at a folk memory of something much, much older. Ritual drowning was a feature of some very old Celtic cultures.

A local rhyme commemorates the event:

On a circle of stones they placed the pot
On a circle of stones but barely nine
They heated it up red and fiery hot
Till the burnished brass did glitter and shine

They rolled him up in a sheet of lead
A sheet of lead for a funeral pall
They plunged him in the cauldron red
And melted him lead bones and all

Behind the folklore is another story. In reality de Soulis was indeed a wicked man. It was a time of national danger when King Robert 1 had removed a truly massive English threat to the country and had stood against Edward Plantagenet who was one of the ogres of history. Now de Soulis joined an English-backed conspiracy to assassinate King Robert. Perhaps history equated the treason of de Soulis to some form of devil-worshipping black magic and treated him as such. Rather than die in a pot of boiling lead-and-water, de Soulis was arrested and placed in Dumbarton Castle. Of course there could have been a different de Soulis who also abducted children; in Liddesdale anything was possible.

However redcaps are not the only supernatural creatures to infest the Border castles, for there are also the Dunters, who are believed to be a folk memory of the blood sacrifices that were made when the foundations of these places were laid.

After the demise of de Soulis, there was still no peace at Hermitage. When King Robert died the English again invaded and captured the castle. They held it until 1338 when William Douglas, the well-named Dark Knight of Liddesdale retook it for Scotland. Douglas was bold in battle but shady in character; he captured a fellow patriot, Ramsay of Dalhousie, and starved him to death in the dungeons of Hermitage, and then turned traitor himself; Scotland was often ill-served by those who should have been her leaders. In turn the Scots killed him in 1353.

Hugh de Dacre was next, and he started the stone-built castle that can be seen today. To judge by the essential grimness of the structure, de Dacre was a man with a guilty conscience, or a deep rooted fear of his neighbours, which is not surprising given the area in which he lived. The Douglases, however, were soon back in charge, but their patriotism did not match their valour and the king replaced them with the Earl of Bothwell.

It was perhaps the most famous Bothwell who brought some romance to the castle when in the 1560s Mary, Queen of Scots galloped across the borderland to meet her man, James Hepburn, Earl of Bothwell, keeper of the castle. That was nearly the last act of the castle's story for after the Union of Crowns in 1603 the old Border died. Peace brought neglect and the castle began to moulder, with the old grey stones crumbling into history and legend. Walter Scott brought new interest into the romance of the area and in the nineteenth century there was an attempt at reconstruction. Hermitage can be visited as it sits still and sombre within its cradle of silent hills, but the atmosphere can still be unsettling.

The legends remain: de Soulis was able to summon the devil by banging on a huge iron chest, and according to the stories, Red Cap still waits in guard of this chest, which of course contains a fabulous treasure. The brave among us may find this chest deep in the dungeons, where the groans of Ramsay of Dalhousie merge with the moans of the victims of de Soulis. Ramsay, however, also haunts Dalhousie castle in Midlothian. Near to Hermitage is the grave of the Cout of Keilder, another unpleasant local who terrorised the locals. Legend accredits him with magical chain mail that no sword could pierce, so in an echo of the fate of de Soulis, he was drowned in a local pool, known ever since as the Drowning Pool. Some visitors have experienced a strange force pushing them toward this pool, so it is best to give it a wide berth, just in case.

So although de Soulis has long gone, the spirit of evil, in one form or another remains in this much abused and deceptively placid corner of Scotland. To appreciate the beauty, it would be best to visit on a spring or summer morning, but to sense the true atmosphere, come in a November or December evening, just as night is creeping over from the Nine Stane Rig and a rising wind spatters cold rain against the groaning walls of Hermitage.

The People of Peace

Scottish fairies are not like those in other countries. While the usual image of a fairy is a gossamer winged little creature hovering above a delicate flower or exchanging a silver coin for a child's tooth, the Scottish fairy was a thing to respect or avoid. The Scottish fairies were the *sidh*, pronounced as shee, and where they lived is obvious by the many glens and hills with the suffix or prefix of shee. For example there is Glen Shee south of Braemar and Schiehallion, the sacred hill of the Caledonians that marks the approximate centre of the country.

Scottish fairies had a ruler, the Queen of Elfhame, and often interfered directly with the lives of humans. Rather than small, delicate things they were about the same size as humans, co-existed in the same world and had a variety of names. Often their name could not be spoken so they were termed the 'People of Peace.'

F. Marion McNeill the folklorist believed that the fairies were a folk memory of the people who preceded the Celtic people, a Neolithic or Bronze Age race who were the original denizens of the land. These people had small communities often controlled by a queen, lived in small houses built partially underground , worked in bronze but were afraid of iron, kept livestock but did not grow crops, used flint arrowheads and were skilled in music.

There were other sides of the fairies; they moved at night, stole babies to rear as their own, sacrificed to their gods and were skilled in magic. The Scottish fairies were not people that one wanted to cross.

Stories of the Scottish fairies are legion, but fade by the seventeenth century and virtually die out by the nineteenth.

For example there was the Battle of Traigh Gruinart in August 1598. This was a clan battle between the Macleans of Duart on Mull and the MacDonalds of Islay. At one time Clan Donald had controlled all the Hebrides but ever since King James IV removed their title of Lord of the Isles their power had been declining. Now Laughlin Maclean of Duart hoped to wrest Islay, once the power base of the MacDonalds, away from them. The Macleans manned their galleys and invaded Islay but rather than fight them, James Macdonald, a very young man, offered to ask King James VI to arbitrate the case.

Maclean was so sure of his power that he refused the offer, making a battle inevitable. The Maclean army was by far larger, but to counter that, many of the Macdonalds were veterans of the wars in Ireland. The armies met at Traigh Gruinart, where James Macdonald listened to wise council and positioned his men so the sun was at his back and shone in the eyes of the Macleans. The Macdonalds won the resulting battle, with Sir Laughlin Maclean among the dead.

The legend says that before the battle began, the *Dubh Sidh*, the Black Fairy came from Jura to Islay and offered his help to the Macleans, but Sir Laughlin Maclean rejected his offer and added a number of insults into the bargain. The *Dubh Sidh* promptly changed sides and joined the Macdonalds: it was his arrow that killed Sir Laughlin.

The fairies were mentioned in another clan battle, this time in 1395, when the MacDonalds defeated the MacLeods. They fought in Harta Corrie and the MacDonalds piled the MacLeod dead around what is now known as the Bloody Stone. Apparently after the battle the fairies made their bows from the ribs of the MacLeod corpses.

Of all the fairy lore in Scotland, perhaps that of the Fairy Flag of the MacLeods is best known. There are so many legends that it would be possible to write an entire book about this square of discoloured brown and much darned silk.

The Fairy Flag or *Am Bratach Sìdh* is kept in Dunvegan Castle, the seat of the MacLeods in the Island of Skye. It is around 40 centimetres square and had small red spots, called the 'elf dots' by some. At one time there were also a number of golden crosses but time has erased these, if indeed they ever existed. Experts have decided that it was woven of silk from the Middle East, perhaps Syria.

However the legends offer other possibilities. One says that this is the magic flag, Land Ravager that King Harald Hardrada of Norway carried with him in 1066 when he set out to conquer England. One hopes not, for Hardrada was comprehensively defeated at the Battle of Stamford Bridge: so much for the properties of Land Ravager. The Fairy Flag connection comes with the belief that the MacLeods of Dunvegan originate with Harald of Norway. The story of the flag, however does not mention the Norwegian king by name but instead claims that a MacLeod received the flag when he was on Crusade in the Holy Land. That makes sense: there were Hebrideans involved in the Crusades and the Flag is of silk from the Middle East, and dated from somewhere between the fourth and seventh centuries AD. If the two legends are combined, then there could be an element of truth, for Harald Hardrada had served in the Varangian Guard in Byzantium, now Constantinople. In such a position he could easily have picked up a square of Syrian silk that was in time transferred to the MacLeods and to which legends attached.

There is another legend attached to the flag: if the MacLeods are in danger of losing a battle they can display the flag and victory is assured. The same legend also claims that the flag has been unfurled on two occasions and each time the MacLeods were victorious. However there is a limit: the flag can only be used three times and then the magic will dissipate. The first battle occurred in 1490 when the MacLeods were losing to the MacDonalds; they flew the flag and turned the tide of battle. The second battle was at Waternish in 1520 and again the MacDonalds were winning until the Flag was show and victory went to the MacLeods. That leaves one battle to go ... although airmen by the name of MacLeod were said to have carried a photograph of the

Flag when they flew the desperately dangerous missions over Germany in the Second World War.

The Fairy legend has a romantic background. It seemed that one of the MacLeod chiefs, possibly Malcolm the Fat, fell in love with a fairy. They married and had a son, but the fairy people called the wife back to them. The couple parted at the Fairy Bridge in Skye. That night there was a celebration in Dunvegan Castle to welcome in the new baby. The nursemaid joined in, leaving the child alone in the room. Naturally he cried and equally naturally his fairy mother heard the cries, found he was cold, covered him in a square of silk and sang him to sleep. When the nursemaid returned she heard the singing but was unable to see the fairy. Instead there was a voice telling her that the silk cover could be used three times to save the clan in battle.

There are other theories the flag could be some garment from an early Christian saint, which is another possibility. Another, which incorporates both the Crusader and supernatural versions, stated that a crusading MacLeod met a hermit while he was negotiating a mountain pass near the Palestine border. The hermit spoke of a malevolent spirit in the pass that attacked Christians. The MacLeod used a piece of the True Cross and he hermit's advice to overpower what was termed a She Devil, or Nein a Phaipen, daughter of thunder. During the encounter, the spirit prophesised the future of the MacLeods and gave him her girdle, which in time became the Fairy Flag. There are a number of other versions.

One of the other better known fairy tales is centred on a minister of Aberfoyle in the Trossachs, who in 1691 wrote *The Secret Commonwealth of Elves, Fauns and Fairies*, not the sort of subject expected from a minister of the cloth. But Robert Kirk was not a normal church minister. According to legend, he was a seventh son and was blessed, or cursed, with second sight. He was also a scholar who translated the Psalms into Gaelic. In his book he described the fairies as somewhere between humans and spirits; they looked like humans and some walked the earth in the guise of mortal men. Indeed they had 'apparel and speech like that of the people and country under which they live' and 'they speak little, and that by way of whistling.'

Kirk was the minister of Aberfoyle Kirk, which is now a ruin but which retains an atmosphere of the uncanny, for these who have the power to feel. Near the kirk was Doon Hill, which the locals claimed was a *Dun Sidhean*, a fairy hill. Kirk was fascinated by this hill, walking the slopes and even lying on top, listening to the sounds he claimed to hear coming from within. Every day, Kirk was said to walk up Doon Hill, and on 14th May his body was found on the route of his habitual walk. Sudden death, through heart attack or other natural causes was not unusual, but there were those who believed that Kirk was not dead but had been transported into the fairy realm that he knew so well. However things now became a little interesting. Although he was apparently dead, Kirk ordered one of his relations to inform Graham of Duchray that he was 'not dead, but a captive in Fairyland. When the posthumous child, of which my wife has been delivered since my disappearance, shall be brought to baptism, I will appear in the room, when, if Duchray shall throw over my head, the knife or dirk which he holds in his hand, I may be restored to society; but if this opportunity is neglected, I am lost forever.'

The message was passed on to Duchray, who was present at the baptism, where sure enough, the late Rev. Kirk appeared. However Duchray was too surprised to throw his knife and Kirk vanished with a look of sick dismay. No doubt he is still trapped in the land of fairy. A large tree on Doon Hill is known as the Minister's Pine and his spirit is said to be trapped within.

Kirk's disappearance occurred at the same period of the Salem witch trials in Massachusetts. It was a time of spiritual upheaval.

Of course all this fairy talk was hundreds of years ago ... was it not? Scotland may be at the forefront of oil development, of medical advances and of technological breakthroughs, but just one scratch from the surface some of the old beliefs can be found.

As recently as 2005 there was a furore when a property developer tried to move a stone that was strong with fairy folklore. St Fillans in Perthshire is a quiet village at the eastern edge of Loch Earn. It is popular with holidaymakers, so a rash of caravans now spreads along the side of the loch, overlooking the island where Clan Neish had as a headquarters and refuge.

It is also a fine place for commuters, so in 2005 Marcus Salter, a property developer with Genesis Properties decided to build a number of luxury properties here. However there was a large boulder in the middle of the site, so Genesis thought it best to uproot the boulder and locate it at the entrance to his estate, possibly with the name of the development written across it.

The locals objected: strongly. As the mechanical digger approached the boulder, one of the local people rushed up: 'Don't move that rock,' he said, 'you'll kill the fairies.'

It is unlikely that the driver of the digger had ever been faced by such an objection in his life. All credit to the company, they altered their procedures as they received a spate of phone calls with the same message. Genesis began to dig near the rock without actually touching it: and the council came into the act. Jeannie Fox the Council Chairperson said she could not be sure that fairies 'live under that rock' and she had been informed that the rock had 'historical importance.' She also said that 'people do believe that standing stones and large rocks should never be moved.'

The rock was not moved. The estate was built around it. The fairies won that round, hands down.

Goblin Ha'

East Lothian is one of the most pleasant areas of Scotland. Situated in the sunny south east, it is a county of fertile fields, smiling beaches and pleasant, historic towns. Yet this area also has its share of battlefields, castles and mysteries. The coast is ringed with castles: Dunbar, Tantallon, Dirleton, while inland is Hailes and the remains of the enigmatic Goblin Ha.

Today the Goblin Ha is best known as a friendly hotel in the picturesque village of Gifford, but the hotel's name comes from the nearby thirteenth century Yester Castle. This castle is not the easiest to find as the remains lurk in thick woodland. However, although there are some walls, the most interesting feature is underground; the cellar or perhaps dungeon that created the name of Goblin ha- Goblin Hall. This chamber is around thirty-seven feet long and thirteen wide with a nineteen foot high vaulted roof. There is a further flight of steps nearby, leading to a well and smaller chamber.

That naturally raises the question: who or what was the goblin? According to legend, the first owner of Yester Castle around the middle of the thirteenth century was Sir Hugo de Gifford. Sir Hugo was a warlock, and the devil granted him an army of goblins who built the castle, including the cellar.

Once the cellar, or underground chamber, was created, Sir Hugo was said to spend much of his time there practising black magic and worshipping the devil. Perhaps he did, of course, but possibly the local people had never seen foreign masons and architects who built the castle with skills knew to that part of Scotland but common to the Middle East and brought to Europe by returning Crusaders.

Yester Castle was built on a promontory formed by the confluence of the Gamuelston burn and the Hopes Water. The walls of the castle followed the two waterways, so it was triangular, and when a moat was dug in front, the castle was certainly formidable. All the same King Robert I destroyed it during the Wars of Independence to deny its use by the English.

Although Gifford is an imported name, *Yester* seems to belong to the locality. It may have derived from the Celtic or British *Ystrad* which means a strath. That would make some sense as Gifford sits in the lee of the Lammermuir Hills. By the end of the eleventh century Norman influence was infiltrating old Celtic Scotland in the wake of King Malcolm's marriage to Margaret. Their great-grandson, William, continued the process. He was the king who adopted the rampant lion as his emblem, thus earning himself the name of King William the Lion. Despite his name, King William was no great warrior, although he was Scotland's longest reigning mediaeval king. He was also so headstrong in battle that he charged an English army virtually single handed, got himself captured and only regained his kingdom by agreeing to pay homage to the king of England. When not occupied in losing his throne, William fought his own subjects, modified the laws and gave lands to sundry Norman-English. One was the ancestor of Hugo de Giffard. Naturally, Scotland being what she is, there is an alternative story that says that King David I, the son of Saint Margaret, granted the land to the Giffards.

Whichever monarch granted the lands, the Giffards prospered in that fertile quarter of Scotland and by Sir Hugo's time, they were high up the pecking order. Sir Hugo himself was an advisor to the young Alexander III, one of the best of Scotland's medieval kings, a relationship that appears to have continued when Alexander reached adulthood. The king visited Yester Castle in 1278, when he wrote to that true ogre, Edward Plantagenet of England. By that year Sir Hugo already had his reputation as a magician who delved into the black arts. He was known as the Wizard of Yester.

In the middle of the fourteenth century Joanna, the last of the Giffards, married Sir William Hay of Locherwart- now Borthwick- and the Hays took over Yester. John, 4th Lord Hay held the castle against an English attack during the Rough Wooing of 1547 but that was Yester's final fling with history. A decade later the castle was abandoned in favour of a new building and the fabric gradually deteriorated, with locals aiding the process by quarrying the stones for other buildings.

There is another legend associated with the Goblin Ha' and that is the Colstoun Pear. The story goes that when Margaret, the daughter of Sir Hugo got herself engaged to Broun of Colstoun, Sir Hugo picked a pear and handed it over. It was a simple gift but came with a condition. The pear had to be cared for down the generations. If it was kept in good condition, all would go well with the Broun family. If, however that pear was damaged in anyway, calamity would follow. Knowing of the power of the wizard Giffard, the Brouns placed the pear in a silver box and all was well.

The centuries wore on, the pear remained perfect within its box and the Brouns remained intact and prosperous, until 1692. This was a bad period for Scotland with the 1689 Jacobite Rising recently quelled in blood and bitterness and the Darien Disaster and years of disease, famine and dearth on the near horizon. Sir George Broun was about to marry his fiancé when she took a fancy to the pear. Taking the fruit out of the casket, she realised that it still looked fresh and took a tentative bite – does that sound familiar? A Scottish Adam and Eve?

The results can be predicted. The previous good fortune of the Brouns seeped away as Sir George took to gambling and lost heavily. Bankrupt, he sold the estate to his brother, Robert, who, together with both his sons, drowned when the River Tyne burst its banks. Sir George died in 1718, alone and penniless. Once exposed to fresh air, the pear hardened and the teeth marks remained for centuries.

Once again, there is another version of the story. This one claims that George Broun married Marion Hay in the sixteenth century and

Marion carried the pear as her dowry. The contemporary Lord Yester said that the pear had to be preserved to maintain the family's good fortune. According to Sir Thomas Dick Lauder it was a pregnant wife of the Broun family who bit into the pear and after that the Broun's fortunes collapsed.

Whichever version is believed, the end result was much the same.

There are other snippets to add to the legends of the Goblin Ha. One is the vanished village of Bothans that lay somewhere amongst the woodland. It was demolished in the seventeenth century and the present planned village of Gifford built in its place. Finally and inevitably there are the ghosts. People walking through the woods have heard voices when nobody else was present, and there are sinister tales of black masses being held in the Goblin Ha, while the ruins are also said to be cursed. It is possible of course, that Walter Scott's mention of the wizard in *Marmion* has helped perpetuate the stories.

Borthwick Castle

Not far south of Gorebridge in Midlothian, Borthwick Castle stands nearly complete, a twin towered monument to the fifteenth century with all the modern conveniences of the twenty-first. When Lord Borthwick brought the king back to Scotland after he suffered eighteen years imprisonment in England, His Majesty gave him a charter to create a castle. The result was Borthwick Castle, with walls up to twenty feet thick.

Built in 1430, the castle has played host to many notable visitors, including the ubiquitous Mary, Queen of Scots and the infamous Oliver Cromwell. There are also a number of stories, such as the tale that prisoners were dragged up from the dungeons and made to jump from the top of one tower to the other. Naturally most were fell, possibly onto spikes below.

There are at least two ghosts said to frequent the castle, and possibly three or four.

The saddest ghost is that of a local girl named Ann Grant. One of the Lord Borthwicks inveigled her with his position and power, promised her the earth and seduced her. Once the evil act had been done, Ann fell pregnant and hoped that His Lordship would keep his word. However, rather than meet her at the altar, Lord Borthwick had her imprisoned inside the Red Room, away high up in one of the towers.

From then on it was all downhill for Ann. His Lordship held her prisoner for a while, and then decided that in her present condition she was more a liability than an asset. Accordingly he sent in a group of assassins. Chopped to pieces so that the room was red with her blood, Ann and her unborn child were stuffed inside the hollow walls of the room. However, she remained as a ghost, with people seeing shapes in the fireplace, hearing scratching sounds and what they thought was a cover being dragged from a bed. Occasionally women sleeping in this room have felt somebody tugging at them, and one lady saw a young woman sitting at the foot of her bed. The lady claimed that the woman told her about the loss of her child. On the other hand, men sleep very soundly indeed in the Red Room, almost as if Ann had made them unconscious to allow her to contact the female guests. In time Ann's presence grew so persistent that a priest arrived to exorcise her. Hopefully she is now at peace.

The second ghost was a little more deserving of his fate. He was a chancellor of the castle who thought that more of the proceeds of the Borthwicks' lands should be in his pocket that was officially allowed. The Borthwicks were not of the same opinion and ambushed him on his journey from Edinburgh to the castle. Rather than a simple murder with the sword, the Borthwicks burned the embezzler to death. He has been seen haunting the Great Hall of the castle and sometimes on the spiral staircase.

The ghost of a red-bearded man holding a sword has also been seen, although nobody is certain who he may be, unless it is a separate manifestation of the chancellor.

In common with many castles throughout Scotland, Borthwick Castle hosted Mary, Queen of Scots. In 1567 she and her new husband, James Hepburn, the Earl of Bothwell arrived at the castle. The queen's nobles, unhappy at their recent wedding, sent a small army to upset their happiness. There seemed no way out for the tall red haired queen until she dressed herself as a page boy and together with Bothwell slipped out a window by a rope, climbed down to the ground and escaped. She has occasionally been seen stalking the halls in her page-boy disguise.

Cromwell was also here, setting his cannon on the old castle during his destructive visit to Scotland. Borthwick and his wife fled and the roundheads took temporary occupation. The castle featured briefly in the Second World War when it housed records and archives but since 1973 it has operated as a luxury hotel.

Edinburgh Castle

Of all Scotland's castles, Edinburgh is perhaps the best known and arguably the most haunted. Unlike most castles, Edinburgh's sits square in the centre of the capital city, an impressive collection of buildings and fortifications with a history that stretches back hundreds of years and includes battles, sieges, murders and one of the most romantic small chapels anywhere. Again unlike most castles, it is still used, with a military garrison and a collection of fascinating museums.

It is difficult to miss Edinburgh Castle, as it glowers down on the shoppers of Princes Street like a guardian gargoyle, but to see it properly, it must be visited. A summer's day is fine, when the views extend to Fife and the Pentland Hills and all of Edinburgh is spread out like a well-planned tapestry, but come in autumn or winter, when an east coast haar hazes the grey battlements and there are fewer friendly tourists to soften the atmosphere, and you might feel differently. Then the old ghosts could grumble from their graves and the atmosphere can be grim.

The castle sits on the plug of an extinct volcano, which means that 400 feet high cliffs protect it on three sides, with a steep slope on the east that leads to an entrance that was defended by a massive moat, gatehouse and rough stone walls. Even today soldiers stand guard, watching through expressionless eyes as they wield bayoneted rifles. Their ancestors repelled attacks by English and Jacobites.

Although there has been some sort of building here for thousands of years, the oldest remaining architecture extends a mere nine hundred; Queen Margaret's Chapel was built for Margaret, King Malcolm's saintly wife, in the early twelfth century. Nearby is Crown Square, where the Honours of Scotland sit beside what may be the genuine Stone of Destiny in a fifteenth century tower hard by the 1511 Great Hall of James IV. There is also the Half Moon Battery, built after the Long siege of the 1560s and 70s, but there is as much below, where dungeons held state prisoners and Napoleonic prisoners of war huddled in the Vaults, dreaming of the sunshine of France while they shivered in Edinburgh's dank gloom.

In spite of all these historic treasures, arguably the most atmospheric building is from the twentieth century. The Scottish National War Memorial was built after the First World War to honour the hundred and fifty thousand or so Scots who died in that conflict. The sheer volume of dead shows the depth of sacrifice that Scotland made, but if the maimed, wounded and gassed are added, the real horror of that war can be guessed at. Perhaps this building is where the real ghosts are, locked inside the memory of the names in each Book of Remembrance.

However, Edinburgh Castle has enough traditional ghosts to satisfy the most eager spirit hunter. Some are well documented; others recalled more by legends and tales. One of the latter is fairly common throughout Scotland and concerns the ghostly piper whose notes can still be heard. It was said that Edinburgh Castle has a number of underground tunnels that slope down from the Castle, extending under the Royal Mile that eventually reaches Holyrood Palace. At some time in the past the governor of the castle decided to see exactly how far these tunnels could be explored, so he sent down a piper, ordering him to play his pipes so that his progress could be traced.

For a while everything proceeded according to plan. The piper marched along quite happily, with the people above ground tracing his progress easily enough, until he reached half way down the Royal Mile, the street that extends from the castle to the Palace of Holyroodhouse, when the sound of the pipes abruptly ended. Naturally concerned, the Governor sent down a search party, but there was no trace of the piper, and nothing has been seen of him since. He simply vanished, but occasionally, if the wind is right, the sound of his pipes can still be heard beneath the Royal Mile and in certain parts of the castle as he desperately searches for escape from the hidden labyrinth of tunnels. Apparently there is also a piper on the battlements, although he may be simply a variation of the same story.

Augmenting the piper is a ghostly drummer, whose beats sound a warning of impending attack. It is said that the drummer was first heard in the seventeenth century, when he played the Scots March used by the Scottish mercenaries of the Thirty Years War, followed by a medley of different marches. Each march was said to belong to a different nationality, and heralded the great Civil Wars of the 1640s and 1650s, when all four nations of the British Isles were torn apart by horrific war. It is also reported that the drummer was a headless boy who appeared just before the 1650 attack on the castle. Today the drums are seldom heard, which is a good thing, as they are meant to presage an attack on the Castle. The last sounding of the drums was in 1960, and as there was no attack on the castle, perhaps the drummer was bidding a final farewell.

One of the highlights of any visit to the Castle is a descent into the dungeons, of which Edinburgh has an impressive collection. Some visitors have seen coloured orbs down in these places where once people were held in desperate circumstances. In 2001 Dr Richard Wiseman held experiments in the paranormal in the castle dungeons, and many visitors, who had no knowledge of the castle history, claimed to have experienced strange feelings in those areas notorious for ghosts. Dr Wiseman, however, was not so sure; he thinks such feelings may have other, more natural explanations.

The Vaults held hundreds of French prisoners-of-war during the eighteenth and early nineteenth century wars with France, and it may be one of these men who tried to escape by slipping into the barrow that carried away the human excrement; hygiene facilities were extremely poor before Victorian improvements. It is said that the prisoner was still in the barrow when the contents were taken to the battlements and emptied down the castle rock, so he died an unpleasant death.

His ghost is said to stalk the castle walls, attempting to push visitors over the edge, but an overpowering smell gives warning of his presence.

An earlier ghost has associations with Lady Janet Douglas of Glamis, who was imprisoned in the sixteenth century and accused of witchcraft. At the time people believed in witchcraft, although the major witch craze had not yet come to Scotland from Europe. What made Lady Janet's crime so special was the accusation that she had planned to kill King James V. To obtain information, her servants were tortured, and when they broke, she was condemned to death and burned on the Esplanade, where today's military tattoo performs its annual ritual.

On the seventeenth July 1537, Lady Janet's son Gillespie was dragged out and made to watch his mother being tied to the stake, strangled and burned and although it is said to be Lady Janet's ghost that wanders the castle, perhaps her son is also there after such a traumatic event. Sometimes the sound of hammering is also heard, as ghostly workmen build the platform on which Lady Janet was executed.

Among the castle's other ghosts, there is a phantom dog that haunts the small cemetery where the pets of the garrison lie buried. All in all, this magnificent tourist attraction has a great variety of other, hidden, visitors.

Rait Castle

Now a ruin, Rait Castle is still an interesting place to visit. Rait is around two and a half miles south of Nairn in some of the finest farming lands in Scotland, and seems to date from the late thirteenth century, although the fabric has many later alterations and additions. In common with most Scottish castles, ownership changed with altering fortunes, and, of course, a resident ghost.

It seems that the then owner, a Cumming, or Comyn, had invited a group of Mackintoshes for a feast, with a nasty plan to murder them. The Mackintoshes had at one time owned Rait, and Cumming of Rait hoped to remove these old rivals once and for all. The plan was to sit Mackintosh and his men to dinner in the great hall, then, at a pre-arranged signal, each Cumming would kill a selected victim. Cumming of Rait disclosed his plot to his household, making them swear an oath of secrecy that they would not tell a soul.

Unfortunately for Cumming, his daughter had a Mackintosh boyfriend, so she was trapped between two loyalties. She could not betray her oath to her father, but equally she did not want her lover murdered. The solution was simple: walking to a large boulder, now known as 'the Stone of the Maiden', she related her secret, fully aware that her lover was on the far side and listening to every word.

On the day of the banquet, the Mackintoshes arrived, each apparently happy to meet their hosts, but each with a dirk concealed under his plaid. Both families joined in the feasting and drinking, until Cumming of Rait gave the pre-arranged signal, 'The Memory of the Dead.' Although the Cummings drew their knives, the Mackintoshes were quicker, and there was a general slaughter. Only Cumming of Rait escaped; he fled to the upper part of the castle, where his daughter's quarters were situated.

Cumming had long been aware that his daughter had a Mackintosh lover and realised that she must have warned of the planned massacre. The girl heard him coming and ran to the window, clutching at the window ledge as she tried to lower herself to the ground far away. Cumming of Rait drew his sword and sliced at her, hacking off both her hands so she fell to the ground and died.

It is said that her handless ghost still haunts the ruins of Rait Castle, victim of her own love and her father's revenge.

Comlongon Castle

Given the violent history of the area, any castle set in south western Scotland should be haunted, and Comlongon is no exception. Yet, unusually, there is an exact date of death and name for the castle ghost. It was on the 25th September 1570 that Lady Marion Carruthers passed from this world to that of the spirits by dropping from the tower of the castle. It is said that no grass grows on the spot where she landed, and her weeping spectre is often seen drifting around the castle.

As so often, the background to the story involves a powerful local lord and a tragic young lady. In this case the wicked local lord was Sir James Douglas of Drumlanrig, a nearby landowner who planned to extend his land holdings, and the tragic young lady was Marion Carruthers. She was the daughter of Sir Simon Carruthers of Mouswald, another castle a few miles away. This part of Scotland, so near the English border, is littered with castles, both to slow down any invasion and as protection from local cattle raiders and feuding families.

When Sir Simon died, he left his lands of Mouswald to his daughters, Marion and Janet. Sir James Douglas promptly moved in, becoming affianced to Marion, and therefore having a claim to the castle, but another local lord, Lord Maxwell of Caerlaverock quickly grabbed Mouswald. Border lairds were never renowned for their patience or ability to keep within the law. Immediately, a contest began between Maxwell and Douglas over the ownership of Mouswald.

In 1563 the Privy Council, Scotland's parliament, ordered Marion to Borthwick Castle in Midlothian and ordered her to remain there until her marriage was agreed. Scotswomen, however, have minds of their own and she slipped away from Borthwick and returned to her own area, taking up residence with her uncle, Sir William Murray of Comlongon. When Marion gave half her dowry to her uncle, she hoped that Sir James Douglas might back off, but Douglas pressed his case and the courts ordered Marion to become his wife.

Marion, however, was unwilling to be bought and sold like so much property, so she threw herself from the window and died on the ground below. At that period, suicides were not given a Christian burial, so Marion still haunts the castle, while Sir James Douglas succeeded in extending his lands to Mouswald Castle. Nevertheless, there is an alternative story that suggests Marion did not jump, but was pushed by some of Sir James' men, so the Douglas got the lands he wanted without the inconvenience of an unhappy marriage. Either way, Marion still haunts Comlongon.

Glamis Castle

Situated a few miles north of Dundee, Glamis castle is a visual delight. It has royal associations as the birthplace of the late Queen Mother and is on the fringes of the Sidlaw Hills and the fertile Strathmore. All these things are to its advantage, yet Glamis is also one of the most haunted castles in Scotland, with enough legends and stories to satisfy the most avid of ghost hunters.

One of the legends speaks of a secret room where the Earl of Crawford plays cards, or possibly dice, with the devil in a game that has no end. Another speaks of a lady in white or grey, who was the lady of Glamis, condemned to be burned for witchcraft. A third is the ghost of an elderly lady who has been seen dragging a sack through the castle grounds. Add to that list some night-time hammering, sundry strange sightings, a running man, a black servant, a missing room, a monster, two armoured men fighting and a possible vampire and we have Glamis. As usual in folklore, there is no clear-cut single legend, but a variety, possibly repeated in oral tradition for many years before the stories were transcribed in different places.

The castle itself is not particularly old by Scottish standards. It first appears in historical records as recently as 1372 when King Robert II gave the lands to his son in law, Sir John Lyon, Great Chamberlain of Scotland. Save for the towers, the fabric of the building is nothing like as old. Given the brawling nature of Scottish history, with invasion and feud, plus the Scottish predilection for discarding the old in favour of the new, it is surprising that anything of the original building should remain.

One interesting legend that is uncommon in Scotland says that Glamis is under a curse. The first owner, Sir John Lyon, also owned property at Forteviot, not far away in Perthshire. However when he carried a chalice from Forteviot to Glamis he broke a taboo that stated the chalice should forever remain at Forteviot. Perhaps it was this curse that accounts for the plethora of unhappy spirits at Glamis. It certainly affected Sir John, who was killed in a duel in 1383

The White Lady, or sometimes Grey Lady, has arguably the most interesting story of any of the ghosts of Glamis. If the tales are to be believed she was Lady Janet Douglas, the widow of the 6th Lord of Glamis. Accused of an attempt to poison the king, her crime was judged as witchcraft and she was executed in Edinburgh in 1537, roughly where the Esplanade of Edinburgh Castle is. She was said to be a beautiful woman in the prime of life and died 'with man-like courage.' The audience attending the annual military tattoo sit near the spot where she was burned at the stake. Her ghost is still seen in two places in Glamis, the chapel and floating above the clock tower cloaked in fire. That must be some sight. She is also seen in Edinburgh.

Lady Janet's second husband, Archibald Campbell, was nearly as unfortunate as he died in an abortive attempt to escape from Edinburgh Castle. Her son, however, was more fortunate. Sentenced to death along with his mother, he was given a reprieve until his twenty-first birthday. Fortunately for him, his accuser, William Lyon, confessed that he fabricated the entire witchcraft story and the son was released.

Some ghosts are merely mysterious, with no obvious story attached. For example there is the young black man who is sometimes seen outside the Queen's bedroom. Presumably he was a servant or even a slave, but now is nameless and unknown, far from home. There is also a lady without a tongue who stares out from behind barred windows or floats through the grounds, unable to ask for help. Another of this ilk is the tall man known only as Jack the Runner who is sometimes seen in the grounds.

One ghost that it is best to avoid is the red-bearded Alexander, Earl of Crawford. In his day he was known as Earl Beardie and was notorious for his scheming and violence. As well as a troublesome neighbour, he also joined in the Douglas rebellion against King James II and was defeated at the 1452 battle of Brechin. Known as Earl Beardie or the Tiger Earl, the Earl of Crawford was notoriously cruel. On one occasion he was said to have stripped a black servant naked and had him hunted to death with dogs while the noblewomen watched, laughed and applauded. That may account for the running ghost, Jack the Runner or even the sad black ghost.

Earl Beardie was also known to enjoy a game of cards. On one occasion he was gambling with Lord Glamis and another couple of nobles late on a Saturday night when he was accused of cheating. When his playing companions tossed him out of the room and down a flight of stairs, Earl Beardie, drunk as the proverbial lord, shouted that if Glamis did not wish to play with him, he would play with the devil himself.

When a servant came to help him back to his room, and reminded him that it was now after midnight and it was sacrilege to gamble on a Sunday, Earl Beardie said he would play every day until doomsday. In some accounts of the story his words were followed by a peal of thunder, in others that detail was omitted, but in all a tall man appeared, with his long cloak brushing the floor. When he asked Beardie if he meant what he said, the earl, rash with drink, said he did. Another version has the tall man appearing at the stroke of midnight, with the same question.

The stranger, of course, was the devil and he agreed a wager with Beardie; if the devil won, he got Beardie's soul, if he lost; he handed over a purse of jewels. Staggering to the west tower of the castle, the gambling pair climbed upward to an empty room and sat down to their game. All this time the servant had been watching and now he heard the pair shouting and swearing. Unable to resist the temptation, the servant peeked through the keyhole. Unfortunately for him, the immediate result was a massive blast of light and then Beardie rushed from the room and thumped him for spying on his betters.

Beardie tried to return to finish the game but the devil was gone and so was his soul. When the earl died a few years later, doubtless he would descend straight to hell.

The entrance to the room was blocked and even today Earl Beardie can sometimes be seen through a hidden window, playing cards with the devil until the end of the world as a penalty for sacrilege. His ghost is also sometimes heard, stamping and swearing. What may be equally sinister is that his ghost is also seen near the beds of children, giving an even uglier twist to Beardie's character.

The legend of Earl Beardie's room being blocked leads naturally to the mysterious missing room. Glamis has a story that there are more windows than there are rooms, leading to the supposition that there one of the rooms has vanished That may be the room in which Earl Beardie still gambles, yet there are a number of other possibilities in the twisted story of this most haunted of castles.

One tale claims that prisoners were thrust into a room and left to starve to death. Another says that a monster was imprisoned here, possibly a deformed child born into the castle; the poor creature was said to be half man and half animal and to have lived for a hundred and fifty years. The Mad Earl's Walk on the castle ramparts may add credence to this story. According to legend again, the 15th Earl of Strathmore claimed that Glamis did have a secret and 'if you could only guess the nature of the secret you would go down on your knees and thank God it was not yours'.

Another legend tells of the dark old days of clan battles, when the Ogilvies and Lindsays, always ill-neighbours, had a full scale clan battle. While one side proclaimed victory, wounded survivors of both sides were given refuge in Glamis. The Earl placed them carefully in rooms well apart and did not tell either side of their opponent's presence. He locked them in securely and by mistake or design forgot all about the Ogilvies, who accordingly starved to death, despite their attempts to attract attention by banging on the floor of their room. It was not for many years that their skeletons were discovered, and the sound of their banging can still be heard today. One grisly tale claims that a nineteenth century lord opened the door to this room and found a pile of human skeletons, with some gnawing on their own arms in the agony of starvation.

There is another, probably apocryphal, story that one of the lords of the castle went to investigate the knocking one night. He entered the haunted room and fainted. He never revealed what he had seen. Other legends claim that the knocking is the sound of the carpenters making the scaffold on which Lady Janet was executed.

There are other vague and unsubstantiated legends about Glamis including the idea that MacBeth stabbed Duncan in Duncan's Hall and the story that King Malcolm II was murdered here. As usual with such tales, there is no proof except the long-lasting legend that the royal blood could not be scrubbed away and however often the floorboards were cleaned, the stain returned again and again.

All in all, Glamis Castle must be accounted as one of the strangest places in Scotland. With so many legends, ghosts and dark tales, it is certainly worth a visit by anybody with a penchant for the unusual.

The Piper with No Fingers

This story combines four of the most evocative images of Scotland: a kilted piper, an ancient castle, a clan feud and a beautiful sea-loch. Yet it is hardly known outside its own area. It could be said to encapsulate much of the old Scottish character with a mixture of loyalty and violence, together with veneration for the arts.

The legend centres on one of Scotland's lesser known castles, the eight hundred year old Duntrune. Situated near Lochgilphead on the north coast of Loch Crinan in Argyll, Duntrune is not on the main tourist routes yet in its day it was an important fortress. Argyll, it should be remembered, is the location of the ancient kingdom of Dalriada, the heartland of the Gaeltachd, and was where the Lords of the Isles had their Islay headquarters as well as being the homeland of the Campbells. It was a vital, thrusting area in Scottish history.

Duntrune Castle had its share of historical events, being besieged in 1644 during the great Civil War and burned during Argyll's insurrection of 1685. However for the purposes of this book, its most strange event occurred in 1615, when the Campbells and MacDonalds were at loggerheads. This is not the place to go into details for the reasons, but suffice to say that national politics were involved as well as rivalry for leadership of the Gaeltachd.

As seems to always be the case, there are at least two versions of events. The first states that Coll Ciotach of Clan Donald captured Duntrune Castle from its Campbell owners and put in a MacDonald garrison before sailing away to pursue his war in Northern Ireland. With Duntrune being strategically important as well as being close to the Campbell power base of Inveraray, the Campbells could not afford this insult and promptly re-captured Duntrune. These old clan wars were not known for their mercy and the MacDonald garrison were promptly put to the sword, with the exception of the piper. There is a tradition that pipers, together with harpers, medical men and other learned people, were treated with more respect in the old Gaelic culture. Certainly pipers had an honoured position in times of battle, as they were often in the forefront, the place of most danger, encouraging the warriors to deeds of glory.

In this case the MacDonald piper was allowed his life and apparently even the freedom to wander around Duntrune. He spent some time on the battlements of the castle, and the rest of his days in composing a brand new pibroch, quite different from anything he had written or played before. It was a wild, weird tune, full of symbolism and doom. The piper knew that eventually Coll would return from the Irish wars and the Campbells would be waiting for him, so as he stood on the battlements he watched for Coll's galley sailing up the loch.

As soon as he saw the familiar ship, the piper produced his pipes and played his new tune, blowing away on the pipes as if his lungs would burst. At first his music had no effect; the galley continued to power toward him, with its sail bellying in the wind and the oarsmen hauling away at their oars. However as the galley came closer, Coll realised that something was amiss. He did not know that strange tune and there was no group of friendly MacDonald faces waiting to welcome him back. Rather than steer for the castle, he put his helm about and turned the galley away for a safer berth.

When the Campbells saw Coll's galley turn, they knew that the piper had given his warning. Accordingly they grabbed him and cut off his fingers, the worst possible thing to do to a man who played the pipes. When the piper eventually died from neglect and loss of blood, the Campbells buried him beneath the floor of the castle. His self-sacrifice became known of course, and the pibroch was retained and named as 'The piper's warning to his master.'

That story was regarded as a myth, one of the many hoary old tales that enliven the coasts and islands of the west. That is until the late nineteenth century when renovation work was carried out at the castle. The great stone slabs of the courtyard floor, or perhaps the kitchen were lifted and there underneath was the skeleton of a man, complete in all aspects apart from his fingers. The Dean of Argyll removed the remains and gave it a careful Christian burial.

Other versions of the tale claim that it was Alastair MacDonald who captured the castle during the civil war of the 1640s rather than his father in 1615 and the piper's entire hands were cut off rather than his fingers. There is also an alternative story that says the piper was sent as a spy. Whatever the truth, at certain times, those with the gift to hear may listen to the ghostly piper playing the pibroch once more as he warns his chief that the Campbells have come to Duntrune.

Ardvreck Castle

Hard by Loch Assynt and a few yards off the A837 north of Inchnadamph, the remains of Ardvreck Castle comprise one of the most picturesque and atmospheric ruins in the country. With a waterfall close behind and backed by towering mountains, Ardvreck Castle thrusts its towers skyward in broken defiance, a memory of days of glory, of clan feuds and dark deeds of betrayal.

This was a bitter frontier in old Scotland, a battleground between Norse and Gael, Christian and pagan, MacLeod and Mackenzie, and Ardvreck Castle is a solid reminder of those days. This area of Sutherland was the territory of the MacLeods, a Gaelic clan with Norse ancestry, and it was said that the Devil himself was as involved with the creation of Ardvreck as he was with its destruction. Yet before the MacLeods there were the MacNicols, and when a MacLeod married a MacNicol heiress, he wished for a strong castle in such a dangerous location.

Naturally the devil heard of this desire, and offered to build such a place so long as MacLeod promised his soul. At first MacLeod refused, saying, quite logically, that his time enjoying his castle would be short, but his time in hell long.

There matters stood until MacLeod's daughter entered the scene; she was young and beautiful and was immediately attracted to the handsome man the devil appeared to be. A new bargain was struck: the devil could marry MacLeod's daughter in return for building Ardvreck Castle. Both kept their word, but the daughter was never seen alive again.

However, other probably more reliable, sources claim that Ardvreck was built by Angus Mor (Big Angus) MacLeod in the late fifteenth century. Originally Ardvreck was little more than one of the ubiquitous rectangular stone towers that pinned down the Scottish countryside, but Donald Ban MacLeod later added refinements that included the vaulted cellars that can be seen, but not now safely entered. More buildings followed, kitchens, stables and servants quarters, all within a protective stone wall, until Ardvreck was quite a powerful small fortress.

The defences were necessary, for in the seventeenth century this part of Scotland was massively troubled. It was a time of great religious and political upheaval, culminating in the Civil war that spluttered between 1639 and 1651. When the great Marquis of Montrose ended his military career at the defeat of Carbisdale in 1650, he fled westward, to be captured and imprisoned in Ardvreck by MacLeod. It is easy to blame the chief for his supposed treachery, but that would be a false assumption. It seems that MacLeod's wife had a personal grudge against Montrose, who had killed many of her family in an earlier campaign, and what man can go against the wishes of his wife? It has been said that by betraying Montrose, Niall MacLeod began the destruction of his castle, for Ardvreck, unable to bear the shame of betrayal, started to crumble of its own volition.

There were other incidents, such as the siege in 1646 when the Mackenzies came to call. A small group were back at the gates in 1671, at a time that Niall MacLeod was heavily in their debt. Although the sheriff depute of Sutherland ordered Ardvreck to give itself up, the MacLeods were not yet ready. They replied that they would maintain the castle against the king and all who would take his part, reinforcing their words by hurtling a massive stone at the sheriff.

Not surprisingly, the sheriff hurriedly withdrew, but the Mackenzies sought letters of fire and sword and returned in June 1672 with a much larger force. John MacLeod, with eighteen sturdy men, remained within Ardvreck, with Niall MacLeod hovering somewhere in the hills with a reputed three hundred men, waiting his chance to intervene.

When the Mackenzies demanded that John surrender, he refused, adding that he cared not a plack (a small, almost worthless coin) for the king. Rather than a direct assault, the Mackenzies began a siege, preventing the MacLeods from entering or leaving the castle. When the Mackenzies advanced with cannon, foot and musketeers the MacLeods realised that their mediaeval walls were outmatched and surrendered. For the next half century, Ardvreck was a Mackenzie stronghold.

Another, more colourful version of the tale says Ardvreck began to collapse from the time MacLeod betrayed Montrose, but during the Restoration, Niall MacLeod held a great celebratory ball to prove his loyalty to King Charles II. The ball started on a Saturday but continued into the Sunday, which would have annoyed the staunchly Presbyterian Mackenzie neighbours. To deceive them, MacLeod blacked up all the windows so they would not notice dawn had come, and cut out the tongues of all the cocks so they could not crow. The devil, of course, now entered the picture and spread fire over the castle he had built. Yet another story claims the disgusted Mackenzies set fire to such an ungodly place.

Whatever version was correct, the castle was abandoned in 1728 and has never been re-occupied, save for the ghosts. However, these are many. Perhaps the most poignant is the daughter of the first MacLeod chief, who made his pact with the devil to build the castle. She married the devil, but drowned in the loch and her ghost, continually crying is seen on the small beach beneath the castle. There is also the figure of a man, who appears amidst the castle ruins, but no legend seems to be attached to him, and no description save that he wears grey. There is also a more obscure ghost of a woman who tried to interfere with visitors as she watches the ruins. Finally, the waters of the loch and nearby river are said to contain a large eel like creature, which may or may not be supernatural

Endpiece

So there we have some of the strange stories of Scotland. There are many more. Scotland is a unique nation where legends jostle and overlap each other, where place names and street names can hide a mystery, where castles glower from hillsides and remote lochs. It is a nation where nothing can ever be taken at face value and where the seemingly innocuous can hide anything from a murder to a piece of amazing innovation.

Scotland is the land of Conan Doyle and Burns, of the Howff in Dundee where a grave digger was nearly buried alive, of haunted ships and stone-age villages. It is a place of carved stones and mediaeval abbeys. Only a few of their stories were related in the preceding pages. Perhaps a future book will unveil more of the Strange Tales of Scotland.

Jack Strange
Scotland
January 2017.

Printed in Great Britain
by Amazon

15042058R00092